THE BALANCE OF FREEDOM:
POLITICAL ECONOMY, LAW, AND LEARNING

THE BALANCE OF FREEDOM: POLITICAL ECONOMY, LAW, AND LEARNING

Edited by

Roger Michener

Paragon House

A PWPA Book
St. Paul, Minnesota

Published in the United States of America by
Professors World Peace Academy
2700 University Avenue West
St. Paul, Minnesota 55114

A Professors World Peace Academy Book

The Professors World Peace Academy (PWPA) is an international association
of professors and scholars from diverse backgrounds, devoted to issues
concerning world peace. PWPA sustains a program of conferences and
publications on topics in peace studies, area and cultural studies, national
and international development, education, economics and international
relations.

Library of Congress Catalog-in-Publication Data

The balance of freedom: political economy, law, and learning / edited by
    Roger Michener.
        p. cm.—(World social systems. Liberal democratic societies)
        ISBN 0-943852-73-0 (hc.): $34.95 — ISBN 0-943852-74-9 (pbk.):
    $17.95
        1. Liberalism. 2. Democracy. 3. Political Culture. 4. Economic
    Policy. 5. Rule of Law. 6. Education, Humanistic.
     I. Michener, Roger. II. Series.
    JC571.B338 1995
    323.44—dc20

                                                            94-38254
                                                                CIP

TABLE OF CONTENTS

Liberal Democratic Societies

SERIES EDITORS: ROGER MICHENER AND EDWARD SHILS

Civility and Citizenship
EDWARD BANFIELD

Morality and Religion
GORDON L. ANDERSON AND MORTON A. KAPLAN

The Mass Media
STANLEY ROTHMAN

Nationality, Patriotism and Nationalism
ROGER MICHENER

Work and Employment
DAVID MARSLAND

Democracy in Non-Western States
DENNIS AUSTIN

The Balance of Freedom:
Economy, Law, and Learning
ROGER MICHENER

Liberal Democratic Societies is part of a larger series on World
Social Systems by Morton A. Kaplan, General Editor. The
other systems examined are the Soviet System, series editor
Alexander Shtromas, and China, series editor Ilpyong J. Kim.
These books are available from:

PWPA Books
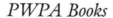
2700 University Avenue West, Suite 47
St. Paul, MN 55114, USA

Phone (612) 644-2809 • Fax: (612) 644-0997

SERIES EDITORS' FOREWORD

Liberal democratic societies, as patterns of political, economic and social arrangements, would seem to be vindicated against their detractors. Until recently Marxism in its various forms and other proponents of single party states and centrally planned economies appeared to offer realistic and allegedly beneficial alternatives to liberal democracy. Events in China, the Soviet Union, Eastern Europe, and the Third World have so reduced the persuasiveness of these arguments that there are no readily apparent alternatives to liberal democratic societies.

Nevertheless, the discomfitures and embarrassments of single party states should not be regarded as a justification for complacency. We should be appreciative of the merits of liberal democratic societies, but we should be aware of their shortcomings, in light of their own ideals, and of the dangers to which they are liable.

The purpose of the present series of books is to take stock of and to assess, in an historical perspective, the most central achievements and shortcomings of liberal democratic societies, and to encourage thought on their maintenance and improvement.

Not only do we seek to delineate some of these main lines of historical development of the variant forms of liberal democracy, but we also seek to discern certain fundamental postulates that are common to these institutions and processes. In this way, we hope to define more clearly the liberal democratic ideal and its limits. We wish to learn where the practice falls short of the ideal or deforms it. We wish to form an estimate of the destructive forces within the liberal democratic ideal itself and of their potentialities for causing its deterioration or its collapse. We wish above all to learn how these destructive potentialities may be averted.

This series insists on the bond between liberalism and

democracy. Liberalism and democracy are two distinguishable components of present-day liberal democratic societies. Their combination into a particular form of society is a great achievement but it is also a source of difficult problems. For instance, can these societies reconcile the fundamental conflict between minimizing governmental authority and intrusiveness and the democratic demand for more governmental activities and greater governmental provision of welfare services? What are the consequences of some of the institutions of liberal democratic society for the daily life of the individual in his or her private sphere? These questions and others like them constitute a continuing challenge for the present and successor generations. These books are devised to assist in the understanding of that challenge.

Roger Michener
Edward Shils

INTRODUCTORY NOTE

Roger Michener

I

The papers published here consider three aspects of the institutional order of contemporary liberal democratic societies, and the role played by this institutional order in preserving, fostering, and maintaining freedom. These are original papers on diverse subjects that have in common the outlook of the institutional order and the purpose of showing the importance as well as the fragility of the institutional order for modern liberal society. To this extent they also address a common question: How do institutional mechanisms, as they have developed in liberal societies, simultaneously preserve and endanger the liberal social order and freedom itself?

Prior to their revision, these papers were part of a much larger and more elaborate academic effort, perhaps the most comprehensive undertaken to date, to show the principal topographic features of liberal societies. Under the sponsorship of the Professors World Peace Academy, the Fourth International Congress held in London in August 1989, had the stated purpose "to take stock of and to assess, in an historical perspective, the most central achievements and shortcomings of liberal democratic societies" and to assay their present state and future prospects. Over several days, the Congress met in eleven panels that involved the presentation of more than one hundred commissioned scholarly papers to nearly four hundred participants. The papers collected in this volume, one of seven in the series edited by Edward Shils and myself, are taken from the three panels devoted to describing the liberal aspirations of specific institutions associated with the relationship between political and economic interests, the realm of law, and the world of fundamental research and higher learning. Being able to bring together essays from such differing perspectives and disciplines was thought also to be an objective of the Congress, namely, to demonstrate that democracy and freedom have a complex relationship to various institutional orders, which, in turn, rely on the processes of regulation, rational analysis, and the transmission of knowledge and discovery.

The final paper by Robert H. Bork, included as an afterword, was presented at a plenary session of the Congress and underscores a theme central to the other papers: the limitations of the liberal ideology and the thought that it may contain the seed of its own destruction.

While the Congress was held only a short while after the brutality of Tiananmen Square in Beijing and just before definitive events in Eastern Europe, the fate of socialism was not a point of reference. Social democracy and collectivistic liberalism, as parts of the liberal democratic tradition formed part of the discussions, to be sure, but the focus was exclusively assessing and weighing liberal democracy, rather than finding a place for it in light of socialism's collapse.

II

The constitutions of liberal democratic societies include provision for social processes that legitimate and preserve the ideal of individual freedom. The approaches taken by various thinkers to discover and understand these processes are closely linked to the history of modern freedom and Enlightenment thought. Some of the most powerful thinkers strove to clarify the place of individual freedom in an interconnected world of social obligation by criticizing older views and creating new ones. For instance, the fatal blow struck by David Hume to the theory of the social contract brought into sharp focus the failure of political and social theory to explain the balance of freedom and social obligation that existed among individuals, status groups and the newly emergent voluntary associations that were a central feature of the commercial and industrial society that stood on the threshold of the nineteenth century. Similarly, toward the end of the eighteenth century natural law theory was subjected to such strong scrutiny that it was no longer successful in describing the moral aspirations of the relationship between the individual and the state. To fill the void created by the deaths of the social contract and natural law, an intellectual tradition of institutional analysis gradually emerged. This new approach acted in large measure as the vehicle that carried along the ideal of freedom after these other theoretical positions were no longer able to do so.

From a philosophical point of view it was, of course, the thought of Immanuel Kant that buried the theory of natural law as it had emerged with Grotius and flourished throughout the Continent until the end of the eighteenth century. And it was also Kant, profoundly influenced by Rousseau (as he acknowledged) who recast the moral aspirations of the individual in the liberal state. Still, Kant was not so concerned with the institutional structures (or the State as Hegel was) that fascinated writers like Tocqueville, who used the experience of the French Revolution and the ensuing Napoleonic period to fashion an understanding that saw society shaped by a dynamic, competitive aggregation of forces and institutions, driven by an inexorable movement toward equality, that simultaneously nurtured and threatened freedom.

A significant theoretical development that helped to explain the developing reality of nineteenth century liberal society—society that recognized the revolutions of modernity and the establishment of freedom as a principle of the modern world—was the German juristic conception of the corporate *Gesamtakt* as distinct from the individualistic *Vertrag*. Enhancing the conception of contract in this way had the notable effect of restoring the idea of contract as an embodiment of mutually dependent and basically equivalent obligations (putatively, at least) and created a modern juristic basis for public law, corporate personality, and the administrative state. It also had the effect of furthering intellectual explanation about the concept of collective entities, or *Genossenschaften,* as Gierke called them. This explanation led to valuable and profound historical and theoretical insights about the reception of Roman law and its influence in shaping modern society. Gierke, for instance, came to see a fundamental dichotomy between the claims of society and those of the individual. He felt that the latter claims were relatively modern, derived from the Romantic tradition, and overshadowed the claims of society. From this starting point he and other thinkers became interested in associations that had received but did not depend upon state recognition for their associational life.

The elaboration of this new theoretical position, in turn, led to a deeper understanding of bureaucracy, state regulation of "natural" monopolies, governmental agencies that administered the collective needs of society, and, generally, what is now called the administrative state. Accompanying this scholarly work was the heightened appreciation of administrative discretion. Few thinkers have followed Albert Venn Dicey in his observation that the administrative use of discretion was, *a fortiori,* beyond the rule of law because it was arbitrary, possibly because they did not wish to draw conclusions about the legitimacy of collectivistic liberalism at a time when that view was clearly ascendant. Nonetheless, as a matter of logic Dicey is correct (and as a matter of reality probably also correct); he and others helped formulate the view that one of the dangers to liberal society was the absolutist and centralizing tendencies of the contemporary administrative state, that, in a world of demands that outstripped the resources to pay for them, employed its discretion to enforce selectively regulations that are too myriad and too complex either to be understood properly or imposed consistently.

While intellectuals of a collectivistic predisposition hesitated to criticize the emergence of the administrative state in liberal democracies as an infringer of freedom, they were quite willing to undertake, often very successfully, an institutional analysis of authoritarian regimes headed by Hitler and Mussolini and of hybridized forms of state control, possibly more subtle and harder to describe, such as the corporatism of Peron's Argentina. This technique of analysis was never fully extended, so far as I know, to Stalin's Soviet Union, but now that archives and records are becoming available, scholarly work might now follow. A recent example of this mode of analysis is Karel van Wolferen's 1989 book *The Enigma of Japanese Power*. Van Wolferen probed Japan's supposedly independent institutions—the political parties, the courts, the press, advertising firms—more systematically and thoroughly than other authors. He argued that they are all part of an interconnected system of social engineering, superior in quality to other twentieth century engineering, that have coordinated social institutions to centralize state authority.

It is under this type of analysis that the complicated and often contradictory character of the modern administrative state is best seen: in addition to meeting the increasingly stringent criteria of equality, the state must simultaneously administer welfare and maintain freedom, individual and collective. Serving these goals simultaneously and balancing social obligation and freedom is patently paradoxical, impossible within the present day structure of the liberal democratic state. Indeed the social goal that is still attainable is to keep the imbalance from growing too great, which, in turn, depends on an interaction with the other institutional orders in the larger society. The institutional approach is particularly helpful in showing where the compromises have been made and where the new directions may be found.

III

This institutional mode of analysis is the common denominator for the papers presented here. The essays of Allan Meltzer and Antony de Jasay consider from the institutional point of view the role of political economy in maintaining this balance—or, rather, in checking the tendency to imbalance—between the administrative state, which seeks its "elective affinity" of fulfilling the welfare role at the expense of freedom itself. The papers of George Fletcher and Andrzej Rapaczynski follow a similar path for the institution of law, as do the contributions of Edward Shils, Walter Rüegg, and Heinz Maier-Leibnitz for the world of science and learning. Political economy, law, and scientific advancement (and its technological offspring) are intimately connected as scholars increasingly realize, especially in discussions about national industrial policy and international trade. While there is considerable variety in the subject matter of these papers as well as in their approach, they have a common and fundamental concern with exploring some aspect of the dangers and antinomies that haunt liberal democracy.

Judge Bork's essay is on a somewhat different plane, but it complements the other papers by pondering the future prospects of liberal societies. His contribution is important for its remarks about the moral core of liberalism, "the emptiness and boredom that lie at the heart of liberalism," and the way in which the institutional order has responded to this profound feature of society. Many of liberalism's classic writers, Adam Smith and Alexis de Tocqueville, to name only two, explored the dimension of liberal democracy that might be called moral enervation, and the underlying social and moral forces that combine to bring it about. Judge Bork has revisited this theme. With great seriousness, he points to the inadequacy of the moral dimension in liberal society and suggests that the *status quo* cannot last. The moral problem is endemic to liberalism and may be in the end its most significant threat.

INTRODUCTORY NOTE

It is hard to say with any certainty if the current moral malaise that Judge Bork points to is a "natural" feature of these societies or if it is a passing condition. Perhaps, as Judge Bork hints, if I read him rightly, it is both. Of course these societies are never fully at peace with themselves, as the recent tension between the principles of equality and individual right amply demonstrates. Indeed, competition among the leading social principles that guide liberal democracies, where one is never fully transcendent over the others, ensures some turmoil. Perhaps the notable advantage of the institutional style of analysis typified by these papers is that it allows the reader to see this competition among liberal principles played out on the fields of society's institutional order—a disturbing sight, occasionally exhilarating.

ONE

VOTING RIGHTS AND REDISTRIBUTION: IMPLICATIONS FOR LIBERAL, DEMOCRATIC GOVERNMENTS

*Allan H. Meltzer**

"Individuals have rights, and there are things no person or group may do to them (without violating their rights). So strong and far-reaching are these rights that they raise the question of what, if anything, the state or its officials may do." Nozick's (1968, p. ix) defense of individual freedom opens with these words. What do the words mean?

As a positive proposition about the limits to government's control or influence over property, income distribution, and the allocation of resources, Nozick's statement is rejected everywhere. In countries where people choose their political leaders directly or indirectly in competitive elections, what government "may do"—its command over resources by taxing, regulating or other means—has expanded for at least a century. Redistribution across groups, both temporally and inter-temporally, is the major reason for the growth of government budgets in developed, market economies with near universal suffrage. In totalitarian systems, where competitive elections are restricted or prevented, as in the former Soviet Union, China, or Eastern Europe, most property rights vanish, and the state is the dominant influence on income distribution or redistribution.

Nozick's proposition also fails as a relevant statement about what governments ought to do, or not do, about resource allocation in practice. The reason is that the proposition has no application to totalitarian societies, and it does not take account of voting. Neither Nozick's statement, nor the book that follows it, proposes a means by which voters can restrict the role of government to activities that do not violate some individual's rights to his property and income. Evidence suggests that no major political group supports Nozick's proposals. In many countries liberal parties that once exhorted voters to protect property rights and restrict the role of government have either declined to insignificance in this century or changed their programs.

The assignment of tasks to a collective body—the state—and the use of coercion has generated a large literature. A problem with much of this literature is that, like Nozick, it does not take account of voting. Near universal suffrage provides voters an opportunity to redistribute property, income and wealth. Once voting rights are granted, voters have the right to redistribute, subject to some limitations in law or custom. Often the limitations are reinterpreted or removed when there is sufficient public support for change.

This chapter takes a positive approach to the role of government in redistribution. In contrast, much previous literature on the role of the state is normative and, most recently, has been written from a constitutional or contractarian perspective. The following section reviews a small part of this literature to highlight differences in the approach taken here. Then, I discuss the process of change and its relation to coercion and redistribution, summarize some earlier work on the relation of voting rights to property rights and redistribution and some implication of that work for liberal, democratic society. Finally, I restate some main conclusions.

Constitutions and Contracts

The future of liberal democratic societies depends on the functioning of the market process, the political process, and the interaction between the two. Perceived failure of the market process, as in the depression of the 1930s, was followed by restrictions on markets; tax rates and redistribution increased; a search for alternatives to the market most often shifted decision making from the individual to some collective body. Perceived failure of socialist economies and sustained growth of the market economies, as in the past forty years, has been followed by increased reliance on individual decisions and the market process. In democratic countries, shifts of this kind reflect the voters' consensus; they are based on the consent of the governed or, at least, of those who vote. A less orderly process occurs in non-democratic countries. Outcomes are less predictable. Physical force has been used to maintain tyrannies, and it is far from certain that force will not be used again in parts of Eastern Europe, as in China, to prevent voters from making social decisions.

A key difference between democratic and non-democratic processes governing change arises from the presence or absence of an accepted constitutional order. An operative constitution specifies how changes in rights and obligations may occur legally, in a way that is acceptable to the relevant group. A constitution provides a means by which citizens can change the allocation of rights, including the right to vote and participate in the process of change.[1]

The theory of constitutional order has been treated in philosophy and in the social sciences, most recently in work on public choice or political economy. In his Nobel lecture, James Buchanan (1987) pointed out that, at the turn of the century

THE BALANCE OF FREEDOM

Knut Wicksell (1958) was one of the first to provide a foundation for choices involving individual and collective action. That foundation has three elements. Methodological individualism recognizes that choices are made by individuals acting according to their own preferences under constraints, including rules or social norms. Economic man posits that individuals make the choices purposefully to achieve their objectives. Politics as exchange treats the political process as a means of achieving private objectives through collective decisions. Wicksell retained the criterion of efficiency as a basis for judging outcomes of the political process, so he favored unanimity, or near-unanimity, in political decisions.

Two of Buchanan's contributions were to revive concern for these issues in economics and to shift the focus of discussion from policy actions or decisions to the rules under which the decisions are taken. Buchanan analyzed constitutions as rules that specify the process by which society makes or changes the rules under which it is governed. If the rules are tightly drawn and enforced, they reduce uncertainty about whether property will be confiscated or wealth redistributed differently in the future than in the past and present. Rules may provide for due process and restrict what governments may do. They determine who votes, how the rules for voting and for changing the constitution can be altered, and how rules may be enforced and interpreted.

A social order that avoids both the tyranny of a minority and mob rule restricts the actions of the government and the governed. By what principles can, or should, such restrictions be established? John Rawls (1971, 1974) proposed two principles that have received much attention. First, Rawls treats the constitution as a contract, voluntarily entered into, that is binding once it is accepted. Second, he assumed that agreement is reached behind a "veil of ignorance"; individuals choose the rules for redistribution before they know their income, wealth or position in society.

Rawls and those who use the Rawlsian approach take a contractarian position. The constitution is the product of a voluntary agreement that is binding on the participants. The contractarian position obviously fails as a positive explanation of the development of states and constitutions. Nation states did not evolve in this way, and constitutions are subject to change. As a normative statement, without foundation in a relevant, positive framework, the contractarian argument lacks a clear indication as to where it applies. If individuals have the right to vote, they can alter their prior decisions, for example by choosing higher taxes and more redistribution in one case or lower taxes and less redistribution in another. Such changes are the outcome of a constitutional process—for example majority rule—that specifies how changes can be made. A very similar process, possibly requiring a super-majority in place of a simple majority, permits voters to change the constitution. If, at some future dates, voters change the voting rule to enfranchise persons who previously could not vote, both the voting rule and the extent of redistribution may change. The constitution is altered by a process that is part of the contract. The normative proposition that this change is unjust neglects prior agreement on the process by which the rules can be changed. And the process by which rules are changed can be changed also.

For Rawls, justice is a state or outcome achieved by a process that maintains the welfare of the participants when judged by a particular rule for redistribution. Rawls' (1971) rule maximized the position of the poorest in society. Others have modified his assumed social welfare function but have retained the veil of ignorance, the contractarian foundation or both.[2]

Buchanan and Tullock (1962) use a concept of uncertainty similar to Rawls' veil of ignorance to develop the case for constitutional rules. Buchanan and Bush (1974, p.153) are explicit that for them the "veil of ignorance" is a positive proposition about man's position when making binding choices of rules. However, unlike Rawls, they recognize not only that agreements may be broken once information about income, wealth or status is revealed, but also that individuals will take into account the prospect that some rules will be broken. Since many different rules for redistribution may be consistent with majority rule, the rule that survives must have some means of enforcement.

Brennan and Buchanan (1985) define a constitution as a set of rules governing procedural matters, specifying rights and restricting the actions of governments. People establish governments "for the purpose of guaranteeing and protecting the rights agreed on in the contract" (1985, p. 26). All members of the groups must accept the contract; the rules are made binding by unanimous consent (*ibid.*, p. 27). A broad agreement of this kind on the constitution creates a public good.

To avoid some pitfalls of the contractarian position, Brennan and Buchanan treat the term "contract" as a metaphor for the process by which the constitution is accepted by the public. They explicitly reject the idea that the contract emerged or was universally accepted at a particular time. But they continue to use the Rawlsian veil of ignorance as applicable to rules. They argue that people choose rules unaware of the consequences that will follow from their choice but willing to accept those consequences.

Actual choice of rules is a continuing process, not a one-time event. There is no need to invoke the artificial assumption of a veil of ignorance to recognize our inability to predict the substantive outcomes that follow from any particular set of rules.

The problems of choosing, sustaining or enforcing rules for redistribution raise difficult and, as yet, unsolved problems of political economy. Notions of justice, equity and fairness attached to some principles for redistribution should be seen as appeals for social consensus about decisions to tax and spend. Without some agreement on the outcome of the voting rule that is acceptable or enforceable and about what is or is not enforceable, it is difficult for heterogeneous individuals to reach a consensus.

In the standard economic welfare analyses of taxation and transfers, considerations of justice and fairness are never explicit. Optimal tax and spending decisions are derived by maximizing welfare subject to a budget constraint. The process of achieving consensus or majority decision and the institutions of government do not restrict decisions. Choices are made by a government of goodwill that seeks to achieve only efficient outcomes. More recent works by Becker (1983) and by Shepsle and Weingast (1984) are part of a growing literature that considers explicitly some of the deadweight losses arising from institutional practices such as the activities of pressure groups and log-rolling in the Congress. Earlier, Niskanen (1971) used bureaucrats' desire for increased span of control as an alternative mechanism generating excess burden.

By introducing relevant institutional features, models of this kind move away from the relatively barren theory of welfare economics. Log-rolling, pressure groups, legislative staff, and bureaucrats are features of democratic government in many countries. Models with these features help to explain why there are pressures to expand the supply of public services and spending for redistribution in many countries. But growth in spending for redistribution has occurred in many countries operating under widely different governmental structures. Since these models lack voters, they do not explain why voters accept or choose redistribution.

Appeal to costs of information does not justify neglect of voting. The reason is that often voters do not require information about the details of specific programs. Past experience can be informative. Upon announcement of programs for redistribution, public education, health, or child care, a voter with relatively high income, or without children, knowing the past, can be reasonably certain that he will bear a net cost. Voters with moderate or low incomes or large families know that their net benefit is likely to be positive. Upper income voters are usually represented by a party or parties that speak in favor of efficiency, growth and incentives. Representatives of lower income voters advocate "social justice" and "fairness," by which they often mean redistribution. Voters' agents, including elected representatives, understand how redistributive programs coerce some voters to incur costs in excess of benefits to provide net benefits to others.

My purpose is not to deny that institutional structure can influence outcomes and encourage coercion and redistribution. As Buchanan has emphasized, the problem is to explain why voters sustain such outcomes when faced with repeated choices. A full explanation must include voter response and the choice of rules governing legislative or administrative processes. Ignorance, myopia, and lack of information are not sufficient to explain why rational voters in many countries have permitted redistribution and taxation to rise from decade to decade for a century.

Hayek has given extensive consideration to the principles of social organization and their relation to freedom, liberty, and progress in an uncertain world. From the *Constitution of Liberty* (1960) to *The Fatal Conceit* (1988), he analyzed these relations, emphasizing the dynamics of change and the role of chance. In Hayek's works, societies evolve in response to unforseen and unpredictable changes. Each new circumstance gives rise to incentives and opportunities that cannot be foreseen in their entirety by anyone, so the consequences of rules or constitutions differ from those that are expected by their authors.

Economic and social development in this framework becomes a process of trial and error, groping and searching, accepting and discarding. In a Hayekian world, search, adaptation, and adjustment replace Rawls' static veil of ignorance. Progress consists of abandoning rules that produce outcomes that restrict the liberties enjoyed by members of the group. Hayek emphasizes that "evolution cannot be just"

(1988, p. 74) if justice is defined as a state or outcome as in Rawls. The environment in which decisions are taken changes; standards of judgment adapt or change. A static rule for income distribution, as in Rawls, will produce different levels of satisfaction and acceptance at different times.

Hayek's choice of liberty as a criterion introduces a normative element; in practice, liberty has not been the only principle guiding change. Alchian (1950/1977) proposed a broader principle for a particular set of institutions. He suggested that survival is the standard by which to judge the success and failure of business firms. Under conditions of uncertainty, distributions of returns from different strategies or decisions generally overlap. Individuals and firms make choices using available information, including knowledge of the outcomes of previous decisions made by others. These outcomes provide opportunities to copy successful strategies or to attempt to improve upon them. Some successful strategies will arise by chance; so copying or continuing a strategy observed to have been successful does not guarantee success.

With uncertainty, some firms' decisions will be profitable by chance, and others will produce losses by chance. Observers, using this information, will make errors—adopting decisions or arrangements that will not be profitable and rejecting arrangements that could succeed. In the long run, the effects of chance are minimized. Successful strategies persist and are profitable. Survival becomes the test of success.

Brunner and Meckling (1977) extended and applied Alchian's analysis to other institutions as part of what they call the REMM model. Resourceful, Evaluating, Maximizing, Man (REMM) makes decisions under uncertainty, using available information. He strives to improve—to maximize utility—given his preferences and the circumstances he faces. In this model, as in Alchian's, long-run survival of an institution is the measure of success. Success of an institution or arrangement such as the firm, the family or a voting rule is, of course, always relative to alternative arrangements.

The emphasis on the long run is critical. In all social processes there are short-run costs of change and costs of acquiring information. Changes are difficult to interpret with precision, in part because it is difficult to control environmental or background conditions, but also because it is difficult to separate persistent from temporary changes in the environment. The social sciences and theories of stochastic processes are not yet able to specify the relevant conditions to be held constant or to identify the shape of the distribution of changes applicable to many choices. In the long run, these factors have less significance. Rules and institutions survive if voters or consumers prefer the outcomes they help to generate.

Coercion and Change

Hayek's (1960) definition of a liberal or free society is a society without coercion. Coercion occurs when "one man's actions are made to serve another man's will" (*ibid.*, p. 133). Hayek treats a free society as an ideal that cannot be fully realized in practice. If unanimity is not achieved, force or threat of force must be used to collect taxes and defend freedom or liberty. Decisions about taxes or defense require some type of coercion to prevent free riders. There is no operational principle that separates free riding from serving "another's will." Friedman (1962, Chapter 2) would limit the role of government to maintaining law and order (to prevent coercion), enforcing contracts, defining, interpreting and enforcing property rights, and providing a monetary framework. He recognizes the problems of monopoly, where technical considerations permit only a single producer, and neighborhood or third party effects, but he draws no general conclusion about the role of government in these cases.

The recommendations of Friedman and Hayek, and many similar recommendations, are normative statements about the properties of a liberal society. In practice there appears to be a conflict between democracy and the requirements of a liberal, non-coercive society. Democracy gives voters some

10

rights to require all members of the community to pay for goods, services and redistribution that some do not want and would willingly forego. Neither the decisions to spend nor the rules or constitution under which the decisions are made can be regarded as a contract freely entered into and to which all have consented. On the contrary, many would like to change the rules and the decisions but they are unable to do so.[3] The only alternatives open to them are other societies with different degrees of coercion, since there are no fully liberal societies in the sense of Hayek or Friedman.

The conflict arises because a liberal society requires near unanimity, and all democratic societies have some type of modified majority rule. Observation suggests that where governments do not allow the majority to rule, force must be used to maintain authoritarian control. Either voters have the authority to exercise control by choosing outcomes or public officials, or they must be prevented from choosing by physical force or threat of force. An authoritarian government that is unwilling to use force gives way either to another authoritarian government or to some type of rule by the voters.

Recent history provides many examples. Stalin used force and the threat of force to maintain compliance with his decisions. In 1989 events in South Africa, Eastern Europe, and China showed that a perceived reduction in the threat of physical force leads to demands for a more democratic government. But China subsequently demonstrated also that the alternative to permitting democratic rule is a system maintained by physical force and the threat of force. The evidence, old and new, is so extensive and well-known that further discussion seems unnecessary to establish that, if they are given the opportunity, people choose to make collective decisions by some type of majority rule with universal suffrage and one vote per adult person. Other rules do not survive.

Majority rule is rarely, if ever, absolute. There are restrictions of various kinds. The legislative branch is often bi-cameral with one chamber based on geographic location, personal standing, inheritance, or some other criterion that over-represents particular groups. The members of the more popularly elected branch may win their seats in the legislature by a plurality rather than a majority, and the districts they represent may not be equal in size of population. The chief executive may be chosen by the legislature in parliamentary systems, by the electoral college in the United States, or by some other indirect method. A judiciary, appointed for life often has power to nullify laws and broaden or restrict their application. Changes in a written constitution, and passage of specific types of legislation and treaties with foreign governments, may require super-majorities. These and other restrictions on rule by a simple majority are often intended to protect minority rights, including rights to property and income, or to reduce the influence of momentary passions or "mob rule."

Differences in the methods of choosing officials and in the organization of government may be important for understanding particular outcomes in particular countries. Observation suggests that majority rule produces income redistribution in all democratic countries; voters do not restrict the role of government to supplying public goods or eliminating market failures so as to equate private and social costs and benefits. Governments intervene with tariffs and restrictions on internal and external trade. Governments impose distortive taxes, subsidies and regulations and supply goods or services that can be produced privately. Education, health care, and pensions are examples of goods supplied by governments in all developed, democratic countries, but governments also collect garbage, treat sewage, and supply electricity in many countries. In each of these examples, and many others, part of the aim may be to redistribute the costs and benefits of the good or service. Often greater efficiency would be achieved if redistribution was separated and private production substituted for public production of the good or service. Governments in many countries also set minimum or maximum prices for agriculture, labor, interest rates and other goods or services.

Again, the redistribution of wealth or income achieved by these programs could usually be achieved with smaller efficiency loss; there is an excess burden.[4]

The evidence, of which these examples are a part, supports two propositions. First, although there are many differences in the detail of regulations and restrictions, there are many similarities across countries in the choice of goods and services that are publicly supplied or regulated. Second, voters redistribute income in ways that are costly. They do not choose least cost redistribution.

Choosing and Changing the Rules

There are two possible interpretations of these outcomes of the political-economic process. Contractarians take the position that the rules are part of a contract to which all individuals consent. Since some vote against these outcomes, or against candidates who favor the outcomes, it is clear that there is not unanimous consent to the outcomes. Further, since it is the rules under which they are governed that repeatedly produce the outcomes they dislike, voters must learn that remedy lies in changing the rules or constitution. Hence, all do not agree to the contract. To assume otherwise denies that people learn to associate outcomes with the rules under which the outcomes occur.

The alternative view of the political process is that neither political decisions nor constitutions are based on unanimity or near-unanimity. All societies have some degree of coercion; the relevant set excludes noncoercion. In democracies "consent of the governed" means rule by a (modified) majority (or super-majority) that chooses and changes the rules or constitution. Those who oppose the rules may still decide to live under the rules in preference to available alternatives. In this limited sense, they may be said to consent. Notwithstanding this weak form of consent, some will work to change the rules.

THE BALANCE OF FREEDOM

Once we admit costs of information and costs of organizing to protest, it becomes useful to distinguish between active support of the rules (or decisions) and passive acceptance. The former uses resources while the latter does not. A consensus in support of rules or decisions includes those who organize and actively support the decision or rule and those who take no action to oppose. In addition, there are those who dissent; this group actively opposes rules or decisions and works for change.

The Vietnam war protest is a recent example. A relatively small number of dissenters worked to change the minds of many who initially did not dissent from the government's position. By focusing attention on their protests, they helped to change many passive supporters into active opponents and, thus, influenced the policy. The dissenters recognized that costs of distributing information can be reduced by marches, public rallies, draft card burning and other activities that attract media attention. The change was not limited to the particular decision. Enough members of Congress accepted the general position to change the policy toward military intervention for at least a decade and to pass legislation like the War Powers Act limiting presidential discretion.

The same process has been used to change judicial decisions. Those who dissent from a Supreme Court decision rarely persuade a super-majority to amend the constitution. There are exceptions such as women's suffrage and prohibition. An alternative is to make an issue so prominent in national elections that a candidate may promise to appoint justices who are willing to reverse the decision. Abortion is a recent example of an issue where strong opinions and active organization by those who opposed the Supreme Court's Roe v. Wade decision had an effect through the political process. Gradually, the composition of the courts changed until the rule was changed. Political activity did not cease. There is now a different group of active dissenters who seek to change the rules without amending the Constitution.

14

These examples provide no support for the contractarian position. People do not unanimously consent to the rules for pornography, prohibition, abortion, school prayer, or war powers. Some favor a constitutional amendment to limit government spending or to require a balanced budget except in emergencies. On these and other issues, there is no prospect of near unanimity. Some live under laws and rules that they oppose. They are coerced to permit and finance activities of which they do not approve or are prevented from engaging in activities that they favor.[5]

At the state level in parts of the United States, and at the federal level in Switzerland, voters can use initiative or referendum to adopt or reject rules. They can change tax rates, spending or regulation, so they can redistribute income. In the 1970s, voters in several states reduced tax rates and limited future increases. In 1988, a majority of the voters in California decided to reduce the price they pay for property and casualty insurance. They amended the constitution by initiative to reduce insurance rates by 20% and to remove insurance companies' exemption from the state's anti-trust laws. The state Supreme Court upheld their right to do so, subject only to requirements of due process and "adequate" profit.

In each of these cases, and in many others, the contractarian position fails and classical liberalism does not occur. In a system based on some form of majority rule, rights and obligations are assigned by the ballot in ways that differ from the classical liberal prescription. Some individual rights are taken away; others are granted by the ballots of a majority.

There are two processes at work in democratic, market economies. One is the market where allocations are made by agreement, and there is unequal distribution of wealth. The other is the political process where allocations are made by majority rule, and everyone has an equal vote. It is not surprising that the two processes produce different outcomes and allocations than either process alone.

THE BALANCE OF FREEDOM

If the voters were unconstrained by incentives and market responses and didn't care about the future, the political process would transfer wealth from the rich to the poor until incomes were equalized. Democratic, market economies do not reach this outcome. The reason is that voters recognize the disincentives in any system of taxes and transfers that would equalize income.

If we assume that people use the same framework to make decisions in the polling place as they do in the marketplace, voters seek to maximize utility by allocating consumption over time. By raising taxes and redistribution, a majority can increase its current consumption, but higher taxes reduce investment and effort, so future income and consumption is reduced. If the majority votes to reduce taxes and transfers, aggregate consumption may increase while current consumption for the majority falls. The political problem is to find an equilibrium that the majority accepts. The idea, from welfare economics, of having the gainers compensate the losers, would make the democratic process of redistribution futile. Instead, the majority choose a tax rate that maintains equilibrium in the polling place and that redistributes income both currently and inter-temporally.

The political-economic process produces a stable equilibrium outcome in many democratic countries, but there is no evidence suggesting convergence to a unique equilibrium tax rate common to all democratic countries. Actual tax rates, redistribution and other features of the political-economic process differ over time and across countries. The political economy model implies that the differences should be related to differences in voting rules, distributions of ability and productivity, past experiences as they affect attitudes to work and leisure, and to the incentives or disincentives arising from regulation, details of tax and subsidy arrangements and the like.

Some examples illustrate how differences may arise. Switzerland and Japan have had very stable political systems. The same party (or parties) has been elected to fill major offices for many years. Switzerland also gives voters the opportunity to vote directly in referenda. These features of Japanese and Swiss political arrangements are consistent with greater stability in the share of taxes and government spending for redistribution than in countries like Germany, Britain or the United States where political parties representing different majorities (or pluralities) alternate in office.

Larger differences become apparent if we compare Belgium, Canada, Lebanon and Switzerland. Each is a small country with major religious and cultural differences. The political-economic outcomes in these countries range from highly stable to intermittent civil war.[6] Farther removed are the so-called socialist countries where political power was concentrated narrowly, and there was a weaker interrelation between the political and economic processes. As tyrannical restrictions were relaxed, people demanded the right to vote in contested elections. Notably absent were demands for a liberal, democratic society that is free of coercion. Even where people have experienced these tyrannical governments for fifty years or more, most proponents of reform seem to favor majority rule and a reduction in coercion, not elimination of the role of the state in the economy and an end to coerced redistribution.

Some Implications

An economic model without voting specifies social or political choices as a possibility frontier showing tradeoffs. To find a preferred position, a social welfare function must be added. In the political economy model with a voting rule, this is not so. The relevant social choice is the decision made by the voters. Once the voting rule is specified, the model generates an equilibrium outcome or path for that voting rule.[7]

I have argued that the main implications of the political economy model are not the kind of outcomes favored by proponents of a liberal democratic society. Government, acting in response to voters, engages in redistribution and coercion. It grants and reassigns rights. Taxes are distortive, and redistribution is not paid in the form most preferred by the recipients, so there are disincentives and excess burdens. This section first sketches these and other results from a body of more formal work that extends the Meltzer -Richard (1981) model of political economy.[8] Then I offer some conjectures about a few issues that have not been analyzed formally.

The key difference in the model between the economic process and the political process lies in the importance of redistribution. To a first approximation, economic activity produces income and opportunities for consumption. Political activity is mainly redistributive. Individuals work and vote. In the Meltzer-Richard model, people differ in ability, productivity and income. Their abilities and their efforts in the marketplace determine their own and society's income. Taxes are proportional to income, and redistribution is equal per capita. High income earners pay more than they receive; low income earners and non-workers receive net transfers. Decisions in the polling place determine the size of the government budget for redistribution and the taxes that must be paid to balance the budget. The interaction between the political and economic process arises through the effects of taxes and redistribution on effort and output.

In the political economy equilibrium, the distribution of income, tax rates and transfers are determined simultaneously. Since decisions are by majority rule, taxes and redistribution are pushed to the point at which the voter (or voters) on the margin achieves a preferred position. All voters with higher incomes prefer lower taxes and less redistribution; all voters with lower incomes prefer more redistribution and taxes. The former may complain about the burden of taxation, the insufficiency of incentives, the excessive amount of redistribution, the demise of liberalism and the triumph of egalitarianism. The latter group has the opposite complaints; they argue for greater "equity," more concern for "social justice" and

18

increased taxation of the rich. Both groups are coerced by the voting rule (and the requirement that the budget be balanced) to accept an outcome that they would prefer to change. Observations suggest that, despite rather common complaints of both types, the tax rate and the share of income spent on redistribution change slowly. In this framework, stability is a consequence of the relative constancy of the distribution of income (or wealth) and of the voting rule.

As in well-known versions of Wagner's law, the Meltzer-Richard model implies that tax rates and redistribution increase with income. Long-term changes in taxes and spending result from higher income but also from changes in the voting rule and shifts in the distribution of income. The first two factors have increased tax rates and redistribution in all democratic countries since the late nineteenth century. Income has increased and the franchise has been extended to all citizens, regardless of income, wealth, property or literacy. In the United States, the spread of the franchise and voting rights to minorities in the 1960s contributed to the increase in redistribution and tax rates in the 1970s. Slow growth and an apparent compression of the distribution of income worked to lower the growth of redistribution in the U.S., and possibly in Britain, at the end of the 1970s.

Many economists, following Friedman (1962), have proposed replacing the current welfare system with a negative income tax that would make cash payments to welfare recipients. The proposal, if adopted, would remove burdensome costs and permit transfer recipients to choose the goods and services they prefer, increasing their utility.

The negative income tax has not been adopted anywhere. Cash payments are typically limited to persons who do not work for reasons of age, infirmity, or unemployment. A large share of the transfer budget pays for in-kind transfers of goods and services such as health, food, housing, and education. Recipients are restricted from trading these transfers to achieve a preferred bundle, although these rules cannot be fully enforced.

An extension of the Meltzer-Richard model (1985) shows that reliance on in-kind transfers ceases to be puzzling in a political-economy model. The appeal of the negative income tax to the recipients of the cash payments is not sufficient to gain adoption unless a majority of voters subsist on transfers and do not work. Typically, voters who work, not welfare recipients, are on the margin that chooses the type of program. In-kind transfers are preferred by a majority of voters because they increase work, output, and tax payments by the recipients. Additional work permits the recipients to buy goods and services that are not received as in-kind benefits. Cash payments of equal value would have lower deadweight loss in consumption but would reduce recipients' incentives to work.

Recent legislation is consistent with the model. States and the federal government have adopted work requirements. Use of an earned income tax credit is intended to encourage more work. Proposals for a negative income tax to replace existing welfare systems are not on current political agendas.

To finance spending for redistribution and other activities, governments use taxes that also introduce coercion and distortions. Progressive income taxes, though widely used, are generally not an optimal type of taxation in economic analysis. Widespread reliance on progressive taxes is puzzling, as Blum and Kalven (1953) noted long ago. Some recent work, Koester and Kormendi (1989), deepens the puzzle by showing that increases in marginal tax rates, holding average tax rates constant, lower average per capita income.[9] Why are voters willing to lower income in all democratic countries?

Cukierman and Meltzer (1988) show that this puzzle, too, vanishes in a political-economy model. The decisive voter chooses the marginal and average tax rates and the amount spent for redistribution. With universal suffrage and mean income above median income, a majority favors redistribution and progressive taxes even if the choice is costly. A majority is willing to pay a positive price to increase its own current consumption.

The implications of this framework are broadly consistent with common observations about the operation of the political-economic process. Voters typically have a choice between two types of programs. On one side are the proponents of "social justice" who favor more spending for transfers and higher taxes on "the rich." On the other are proponents of growth and "incentives" who favor tax and spending reduction. The pivotal voter chooses between these programs according to his preferences and his position in the income distribution.

Observation suggests that generally a majority of voters chooses one view or the other, and it does not shift frequently from one to the other. Frequent shifts in the tide of opinion would produce comparable shifts in taxation and spending. We would observe greater variability in taxes and spending and in the share of income taxed and redistributed.

These shares are not constant, however. At times, there are large, discrete changes in majority opinion. These changes result from shifts in the distribution of income and changes in the level of income. Periods of rapid growth (relative to anticipations) provide new revenues as well as opportunities for political entrepreneurs with new or revised programs. A widening spread of the income distribution creates opportunities for new taxes and increased redistribution.

Although the effects of taxation and redistribution are distributed over time, most of the formal analysis I have summarized neglects both these intertemporal responses and intergenerational redistribution. A common practice in all developed countries is to require the current generation of workers to provide pensions for retired persons. In return, they receive pensions that are paid by a future generation. This rule, or social contract, is clearly redistributive. Wolff (1987) found that for the United States the direction of redistribution for old age assistance was from workers to all recipients, but low wage workers benefited disproportionately.

Cukierman and Meltzer (1989) analyze the political economy of intergenerational redistribution. They find conditions under which rational maximizing voters choose these programs under majority rule. The programs transfer income to the current generation by increasing current consumption and reducing the capital stock. As Wolff found, the benefits go to the current poor whose consumption increases disproportionately.

In the political economy model, redistribution helps to explain why the government provides pensions. There is a critical difference between the government and individuals; legally, individuals cannot leave net liabilities to their heirs. This restriction limits the opportunity for individuals, acting alone, to redistribute from the future to the current generation by spending and leaving debts. Using government debt to finance transfers relaxes the restriction. If the current poor are part of a majority, they can vote for a deficit financed by selling debt. This permits the current generation to increase consumption by raising interest rates, crowding out real capital and by other means.

Political economy models of this kind may be applicable beyond the range of problems to which they have been applied. One example would be an agreement permitting the United Nations to levy taxes by majority vote in the General Assembly. An international tax would be likely to have effects broadly similar to an extension of the franchise. Redistribution from relatively wealthy to poorer countries would increase. Another example concerns the stability of the political economy equilibrium. If available data are reliable, in Peru and Brazil the distribution of income is relatively skewed. There are comparatively many low income recipients and comparatively few high income earners and comparatively large differences between mean and median incomes. Universal suffrage with majority rule voting has proved to be unstable. The political economy model suggests a reason; in Peru and Brazil, the income of the median voter is farther below the mean than in countries with similar per capita income. Votes for redistribution raise tax rates, reduce incentives and thus reduce growth of output and investment. Those with high productivity leave or send their assets abroad to escape taxation or confiscation. Spending then exceeds revenues, the deficit is financed by money creation, so inflation increases. An authoritarian government may take charge to restore stability, reduce spending and inflation.[10]

The World Bank (1988) provides data on income distribution in developing countries. The data are almost certainly crude, and the observations are for different years, so conclusions drawn from these data must be tentative. I have selected countries with per capita incomes in 1986 in the middle income range, between US $800 and $2400. The World Bank does not give median income; instead I have summed the shares for the two lowest quintiles, the lowest 40% of the income distribution. Table 1 shows these data in two columns. On the left are countries that have income distributions similar to those of democratic, developed countries. Using only the distributional criteria, these countries should be capable of maintaining stable voting democracies. On the right are countries that, on this same criterion, may be unable to do so. Also shown, is the year the income distribution was observed. Comparable data are shown for three democracies below the table, two with relatively high income and one with low income.

Many factors other than income distribution affect the survival of democratic government. Yet, countries with great diversity in language, religion, and culture manage to prosper and remain democratic while countries with seemingly greater homogeneity on these dimensions fail to do so. In the left column, we find three types of countries. There are stable democracies like Costa Rica, countries that made the transition from authoritarian to democratic government in recent years, such as Portugal, Thailand and Turkey, and several countries that are now in the process of transition to democratic government—Argentina, Korea, Chile and the Philippines. On the right are countries that have had difficulty maintaining stable democratic governments where competitive elections and majority rule are used to choose political leaders and programs.

Table 1 Share of Income, Lowest 40%[a]					
Year	Potentially Stable Name	%	Year	Unstable Name	%
1970	Argentina	14.1	1972	Brazil	7.0
1968	Chile	13.4	1977	Mexico	9.9
1971	Costa Rica	12.0	1973	Panama	7.2
1976–77	El Salvador	15.5	1972	Peru	7.0
1976	Korea	16.9			
1985	Philippines	14.1			
1973–74	Portugal	15.2			
1975–76	Thailand	15.2			
1973	Turkey	13.5			

[a]For comparison: 1975-76, India 16.2%; United Kingdom, 18.5%; 1980, United States, 17.2%.

Conclusion

This chapter attempts a positive explanation of the prospects for liberal, democratic societies. I define democratic to mean near universal suffrage and liberal to mean the absence of coercion, as in Hayek (1960). Using these definitions, I find that liberal order and democratic processes are in conflict over the distribution of income, rights and responsibilities; the conflict is resolved by different means in different places but never produces a classical liberal outcome.

A positive analysis of political-economic interaction is used to reach this conclusion. In contrast to the more common normative approach, the positive, political-economic analysis does not introduce a social utility function or rely on a social planner to determine the optimal equilibrium tradeoff between output and redistribution. Once a voting rule is selected, the equilibrium combination of output and redistribution is determined by the voters given their relative and absolute incomes or productivities, the distribution of votes or voting rule, and some structural features of the economy. The political economy model can be used to show why voters chose to redistribute wealth or income temporally and inter-temporally, why much redistribution is in-kind rather than in cash, and why voters choose progressive income taxes instead of the non-distorting, lump sum taxes of economic theory. All of these outcomes are departures from a liberal economy; they involve coercion. In democratic countries, the voters decide on the extent of coercion; in non-democratic governments, the rulers have the power to decide, but enforcement may require physical force or the threat of force.

The prospects for democratic government are brighter than the prospects for a liberal economy. The principal alternative to a voting rule is an authoritarian state where coercion, or the threat of coercion, is used to compel agreement. Experience in many countries, including recent experience in Poland, Hungary, the Soviet Union, Romania, and China, suggests that governments that are unwilling to use physical force to coerce their citizens must accept a voting rule under which the public can affect decisions. The voting rule differs across countries, but much history suggests that the evolution, if physical force is avoided, is toward some type of modified majority rule and near-universal suffrage.

THE BALANCE OF FREEDOM

Is the political-economic equilibrium stable? Evidence suggests that if permitted to do so, people choose some form of universal suffrage and modified majority rule. In the absence of major changes affecting the voting rule, output, growth, or the distribution of income, the share of income taxed and redistributed in democratic countries changes slowly. Shifts of the ruling party or coalition typically do not produce major shifts in the tax rates paid and the share of income spent.

The political-economy model implies that the choice of tax rates and redistribution depends on the difference between the distribution of votes and the distribution of income. Mean income is everywhere above the income of the median voter, but the difference between the two is not subject to rapid, major change in developed economies. The analysis suggests that changes in the voting rule that extended the franchise down the income distribution and growth of per capita income are principal forces behind the long-term rise in tax rates and income redistribution observed in developed economies, but changes in the relation of mean to median income have had a role also.

There is less experience with voting for taxes and spending in middle and low income countries. I conjecture that the political-economy model applies there also, if voters are allowed to choose between competing parties or candidates in free elections. Some evidence is presented to suggest that, once established, democratic government may remain if the income of the median earner (voter) is not too distant from the mean income.

The rules for distribution and for voting are constitutional but not contractarian. A majority or super-majority can change the rules. Pressure for change is always present; there are always some who dissent from the rules. Some prefer higher taxes and more spending. Others want lower taxes and less spending. Some would like to make voting easier; others oppose such changes. Some want increased regulation of commerce or personal behavior; others want less. In stable democracies, these differences are resolved by processes that are acceptable to a majority. Usually, there are some restrictions on majority rule, but unanimity, or near unanimity, is rare. Hence, individuals pay for services and redistribution that they do not choose. The liberal alternative is nowhere chosen.

This chapter has been concerned with the determinants of taxation and redistribution and, more broadly, with changes in rights to property and income. The forces affecting these rights also affect so-called personal rights to expression and action. Casual observation suggests that rights to property and income have been restricted in democratic countries while so-called personal rights have expanded. I conjecture that the expansion of personal rights also reflects the decisions of voters operating under the constitution or voting rule. A major challenge for the political-economic model in the future will be to show that changes of this kind are the result of processes similar to those discussed here.

NOTES

1. See Musgrave (1989) and Buchanan (1987) as examples where parts of Rawls' (1971) framework are accepted explicitly.
2. The changes can be toward more or less coercion and redistribution, as discussed more fully below.
3. Living alone, or in a small group, on an otherwise unoccupied island is not a relevant alternative for most of the population.
4. Decisions can require near unanimity, but few do. An example is the requirement in the U.S. Constitution that a state cannot be deprived or equal representation in the Senate without its consent.

5. This paragraph is based on Meltzer and Richard (1981).
6. I make no claim that the parsimonious model predicts or explains all of these differences.
7. The voting rule can be complex in dynamic problems. The judiciary can overturn a law favored by a majority, but the public can influence the choice of judges with a lag that may require decades.
8. Using a very different model, Browning and Johnson (1984) estimated the cost of redistributing income. The net cost depends on disincentives and varies with the elasticity of labor supply with respect to tax rates. They estimate that the cost of redistribution is relatively large per dollar redistributed. For moderate elasticities, Browning and Johnson report the losses to the net payers are more than $9 for every dollar received by the net beneficiaries.
9. For developed countries, they estimate the effect of a 1% increase in the marginal tax rate, given the average tax rate, as a 0.75% reduction in per capita income.

10. The model has no implication about the policies of the authoritarian government. It may choose policies that increase incentives and encourage expansion, as in Brazil in the 1960s, or it may accede to some of the pressures for redistribution, as in Argentina.

REFERENCES

Alchian, A.A. (1950/1977) "Uncertainty, Evolution and Economic Theory." *Journal of Political Economy*, 58 (June). Reprinted in *Economic Forces at Work*. Indianapolis, Liberty Press, 15-35.

Becker, G. (1983) "A Theory of Competition Among Pressure Groups for Political Influence." *Quarterly Journal of Economics*, 98 (Aug.), 371-400.

Blum, W. and Kalven, H., Jr. (1953) *The Uneasy Case for Progressive Taxation*, Chicago: University of Chicago Press.

Browning, E.K. and Johnson, W.R. (1984) "The Trade-Off Between Equality and Efficiency." *Journal of Political Economy*, 92 (April), 175-203.

Brunner, K. and Meckling, W. (1977) "The Perception of Man and the Conception of Government." *Journal of Money, Credit and Banking*, (Feb.), 60-85.

Buchanan, J.M. (1987) "The Constitution of Economic Policy." *Science*, 236 (June 12), 1433-36.

_____ and Bush, W.C. (1974) "Political Constraints on Contractual Redistribution," *American Economic Review, Papers and Proceedings*, 64 (May), 153-7.

_____ and Tullock, G., (1962) *The Calculus of Consent*. Ann Arbor: University of Michigan Press.

Cukierman, A. and Meltzer, A.H. (1988) "A Political Theory of Progressive Income Taxation." Carnegie Melon University. Reprinted in A. Meltzer, A. Cukierman and S. Richard, eds. *Political Economy*, Oxford University Press, 1991.

Cukierman, A. and Meltzer, A.H. (1989) "A Political Theory of Government Debt and Deficits in a Neo-Ricardian Framework." *American Economic Review*, September. Reprinted in A. Meltzer, A. Cukierman and S. Richard, eds. *Political Economy*, Oxford University Press, 1991.

Friedman, M. (1962) *Capitalism and Freedom*, Chicago: University of Chicago Press.

Hayek, F. (1960) *The Constitution of Liberty*, Chicago: University of Chicago Press.

Hayek, F. (1988) *The Fatal Conceit*, W.W. Bartley, ed. Chicago: University of Chicago Press.

Koester, R. and Kormendi, R. (1989) "Taxation, Aggregate Activity and Economic Growth: Cross-Section Evidence on Some Supply-Side Hypotheses." *Economic Inquiry*, forthcoming.

Meltzer, A.H. and Richard, S.F. (1981) "A Rational Theory of the Size of Government." *Journal of Political Economy*, 89 (Dec.), 914-27.

Reprinted in A. Meltzer, A. Cukierman and S. Richard, eds. *Political Economy*, Oxford University Press, 1991.

_____and_____ (1985) "A Positive Theory of In-Kind Transfers and Negative Income Tax." *Public Choice*, 47, 1: 231-65. Reprinted in A. Meltzer, A. Cukierman and S. Richard, eds. *Political Economy*, Oxford University Press, 1991.

Musgrave, R.A. (1989) "The Three Branches Revisited." *Atlantic Economic Journal*, 17 (Mar.), 1-7.

Niskanen, W.A. (1971) *Bureaucracy and Representative Government*, Chicago: Aldine.

Nozick, R. (1968) *Anarchy, State and Utopia*, New York: Basic Books.

Rawls, J. (1971) *A Theory of Justice*, Cambridge: Harvard University Press.

Rawls, J. (1974) "Some Reasons for the Maximum Criterion," *American Economic Review, Papers and Proceedings*, 64 (May), 141-6.

Shepsle, K. and Weingast, B. (1984) "Political Solutions to Market Problems." *American Political Science Review*, 78, 417-34.

Wicksell, K. (1958) *Finanz Theoretische Untersuchungen* translated in *Classics in the Theory of Public Finance*, R.A. Musgrave and A.T. Peacock, eds. London: Macmillan, 72-118.

Wolff, N. (1987) *Income Distribution and the Social Security Program*. Ann Arbor: UMI Research Press.

World Bank (1988) *World Development Report*, Washington.

*I have benefitted from many discussions with Karl Brunner and Scott Richard of many years. An earlier version was published as the Introduction to *Political Economy*, Oxford University Press, 1991.

TWO

THE BITTER MEDICINE OF FREEDOM

Anthony de Jasay

From the romantic age of political philosophy, many stirring images have come down to us. Some depict a people wrenching its freedom from the clutches of oppressors, native or foreign. Others show the lone individual fighting for his spiritual autonomy and material independence against totalitarian encroachment. Whatever the truth of these images in the past, their relevance for the present is fading. The issue of freedom in our civilization is changing its character. It is not so much despots, dictators or totalitarian creeds that menace it. In essence, we do.

It is far from evident that democratic control of government is usually conducive to the preservation of liberal practices and values, let alone to their enhancement. Anti-liberal ideologies gain and retain credence inasmuch as they suit our inclinations, legitimize our interests and warrant our policies. We love the rhetoric of freedom-talk and indulge in it beyond the call of sobriety and good taste, but it is open to serious doubt that we actually like the substantive content of freedom. On the whole we do not act as if we did. I shall presently be arguing that it is an austere substance, not unlike bitter medicine that we do not naturally relish—though it can become an acquired taste for the exceptional individual but take only when the need presses. My object is to show that contrary to the sweetness-and-light views of freedom, it is this more austere view that best explains why we keep praising it while in our politics we are busily engaged in shrinking its domain.

Taking Freedom Easy and In Vain

Countless notions of greater or lesser woolliness attach to freedom, and a full review of its alternative definitions would be tedious. The very limited sample I choose to look at, however, seems to me representative of the main live political currents of the age. The context of each is non-Robinsonian, in that it deals with a person's freedom as constituted by the options and constraints of his social life. The subject, in other words, is not the individual facing his Creator, nor the solitary player in the game against Nature, but the person acting with or against other persons. The freedom in question is a property of one's conduct in relation to the conduct of others, rather than an affirmation of free will, "inner" freedom or some other proposition about the causation of human actions or the state of men's minds.

The rudiments of the liberal definition identify a free person as one who faces no man-made obstacles to choosing according to his preferences, provided only that his doing so does not cause a tort to another person. This idea of freedom takes preference and choice conceptually for granted, does not worry about how preference can be recognized unless it is revealed by choice, nor does it seek to make statements about the nature of the self. It is practical political freedom. This, however, means something far more general than conventional "political liberty," i.e. the freedom of each to affect collective decisions to some albeit minimal extent through a regulated political process, and normally understood to consist of the freedoms of speech, assembly, press and election. Instead, it is political in the broader sense that it results from the political process, depending as it does on collectively imposed institutional restrictions of greater or lesser stringency on the opportunity set open to choice. As Frank Knight put it, it is coercion and not freedom that needs defining.[1]

By extension of this view, the corollary of freedom is said to be the reduction of coercion "as much as is possible"[2]; in the same vein, it is independence from the "arbitrary will" of another.[3] Giving the matter an ethical dimension, freedom is represented as a state of affairs that permits one to choose any feasible option provided that his doing so does not harm another person.[4] Loosely related to the principles of *non-coercion, independence* and *no-harm*, is the Kantian principle of "equal liberty." It appears to refer to a state of affairs where one person's options are not subjected to a man-made restriction to which those of any other person are not also subjected. This formulation, however, is incomplete. Needless to say, neither Kant nor those, notably Herbert Spencer, who followed him in employing this form of words, meant that the "extent" or "quantity" of freedom in a state of affairs was irrelevant and only its "distribution" needed to be of a certain kind—i.e. "equal." If such a distribution were the sole criterion, it would not matter how much or how little there was to be had, as long as everybody had as much or as little as everybody else. That freedom demanded to be both "maximized" and "distributed equally," was made explicit by Rawls in his adaptation of Kant's principle.[5]

In these versions, freedom appears as a unitary concept. It may or may not be capable of variation by degrees. Hayek suggests more than once that it is indivisible; it is either present or absent; we either have it or we do not; we either choose freely or we are coerced. The "size" of the feasible, uncoerced opportunity set does not affect the issue, nor does coercion vary in extent or intensity.[6]

Liberals of the orthodox tradition, for whom it is a property of the relation between individual preference and choice—a relation devoid of obstacles erected by politics except where such obstacles serve to shelter the freedom of others—do not as a rule recognize a plurality of freedoms. The plural usage, on the other hand, is fairly typical of heterodox, "redistributor" liberals who deal in numerous freedoms to accede to desirable states or activities, designated as "positive," as well as in "freedom from" hunger, want, insecurity and other undesirable conditions. Dewey's freedom as "power to do" also belongs to this category, where diverse "freedoms" represent power to do diverse things. It is not hard to appreciate that these heterodox freedom concepts are in essence rhetorical proxies standing for diverse goods, some tangible and others intangible, that are perfectly recognizable under their everyday names and need not be described indirectly in the guise of "freedoms." Freedom from hunger is an oblique statement about food being a good, and about a condition in which one is not deprived of it; it can be turned into a general norm under which none must be deprived of it. Similarly, freedom of worship conveys, positively, that it is good for each to be able to profess his own faith, and normatively that none must be deprived of access to this good. Employing freedom-speak in discussing various goods can at best underline the importance we attach to them; at worst, it confuses issues of autonomy and coercion with issues of wealth and welfare. The term freedom in the classical sense seeks to express—whether successfully or not—the unhindered transformation of preference into action, the ability of each to do as he sees fit. "Freedom to" and "freedom from," on the other hand, seem to refer to the extent to which options to act are available to satisfy individual or even "social" preferences.

In a spectacular logical leap which speaks well of his insight if not of his talents of lucid explanation, Marx "unmasks" the liberal foundation of freedom: "The practical application of the right of man to freedom is the right of man to private property."[7]

Antagonistic to liberal inspiration, he turns to wholly different categories to construct a concept of freedom. The

Marxist concept has nothing—or nothing explicit—to do with the passage, unobstructed or not, from individual preference to chosen action, a passage of which private property is the privileged vehicle. The corollary of Marxist freedom is not the absence of coercion of the individual by his fellow men through the political authority, but escape from the realm of material necessity, from the tyranny of things.[8] Its subject is not the individual, but mankind.[9] Self-realization—"re-humanization"—of the latter from the "reified" social relations of "commodity production" *is* the state of freedom.

To the extent that this thickly metaphoric language is intelligible, it seems to mean that humanity is free when, no longer subjected to the unconscious and impersonal force of things, which is Marx's code name for the automatism of a market economy, it collectively masters its own fate by deliberate, rational planning. The passage from the realm of necessity to that of freedom is both the cause of, and is caused by, the passage from the realm of scarcity to that of plenty.

Vacuity and Moral Truism

One common feature shines luminously through these various concepts, definitions and normative principles of freedom. Each as it stands is a moral truism, impossible to dispute or reject because each is defined, if at all, in terms of indisputable superiority. Each, moreover, is defined in terms of conditions whose fulfillment cannot be empirically ascertained—when is coercion at its "possible minimum"? —when is man not subject to the "tyranny of things"? The proposition that a state of affairs is free is rendered "irrefutable," "unfalsifiable." Each, finally, expresses a condition which, if it prevails, one can enjoy without incurring any costs in exchange. Consequently, the question of trade-offs does not arise and it would be lunatic to say, with regard to any one of the rival concepts, that on balance one would rather not have it. Renunciation of freedom, so defined, would not bring any compensating benefit either to the self or to others, nor reduce any attendant sacrifice or disadvantage. Unlike values we buy by giving up some comparable value, it is always better to get and keep such freedom than to give it up.

No great analytical effort is needed to see that freedom concepts have this apple-pie-and-motherhood feature when they are vacuous, their stated conditions being impossible either to violate or to fulfill. They make no identifiable demand on anyone and lack any content one could disagree with. That coercion should be reduced "as much as possible" is, *pace* Hayek, a vacuous precept unless integrated into a stringent and clear doctrine of "necessary coercion."[10] Only then would the precept get any definite meaning, for only then would it be referring to some recognizable standard or measure of how far it is "possible" to reduce coercion, and only then could it identify the actual level of coercion as higher than necessary. Otherwise, any level could be as compatible with freedom as any other, and the most shamelessly intrusive dictators of this world would all be recognized as libertarians doing the best they could to avoid unnecessary coercion.

Immunity from the "arbitrary will" of another is similarly empty, for the will of another is judged arbitrary or not, according to the reasons the judge imputes to it. If another's decision rests on identifiable reasons, it may be unwelcome to me because it restricts my ability to act as I would, but I can only have a good claim to immunity from it in the name of my freedom if I have a valid argument to rule out those reasons. Bad reasons leave the decision unjustified, and absence of reasons makes it arbitrary—surely a relatively rare case. Manifestly, however, the crux of the problem is that the claim to immunity from the will of another stands or falls with somebody's judgement of the reasons for the latter; and lest his judgement itself be arbitrary, it must be guided by an independent system of laws, customs, moral principles and whatever else goes into the determination of a person's liberties in his dealings with others. Immunity from the "arbitrary" will of another seems to mean no more than that one's liberties must be respected; its use to define freedom is simply a recourse to a tautologous identity between it and the non-violation of liberties—whatever they are—whereas a meaningful definition should be capable to serve as a determinant, or more loosely as an argument about what those liberties ought to be. However, the rule that in a state of freedom nobody should be subject to the arbitrary will of another, does not commit anybody to anything beyond respecting well-defined rules of tort. It may in fact be that the immunity concept of freedom and the normative rule it provides is even more trivial than that, for it could be held that in these matters liberties are well-defined only if they are codified, and the rule then boils down to the banality that in a state of freedom nobody should break the law.

The harm principle turns out, on inspection, to lack specific content for much the same reason as the immunity principle. Under it, the political authority in a state of freedom does not prevent—or "artificially" raise the cost of—acts that are harmless to others; it does not allow anyone to interfere with the harmless acts of others; and prevents and sanctions harmful acts. However, there is no very evident binary division of acts into a harmful and a harmless class.[11] Some of our acts may possibly be beneficial or at worse indifferent to everybody else, though it would no doubt be hard to make sure that this was the case. As regards these acts, there is a clear enough reason why we should be left free to commit them. But this does not take liberty very far. For there is a vast number of other acts that are harmful to somebody to some degree, having as they do some unwelcome effect on somebody's interests, ranging in a continuous spectrum from the merely annoying to the gravely prejudicial.

This must be so for a variety of reasons, the simplest one being that in any realm of scarcity—scarce goods, crowded *Lebensraum,* limited markets, competitive examinations, rival careers, exclusive friendship, possessive love—one person's chosen course of action preempts and prejudges the choices of others, sometimes helpfully but mostly adversely. The place and the prize one gets is not available to runners-up, no matter how badly they want or "need" it. Where does "harm" to them begin? Common sense tells us that, depending on circumstances, there are acts you must be free to engage in even though they harm my interests, hurt my feelings or expose me to risk. How to tell these acts from those which are to be prevented? Define them, and you have defined the rights that may be *exercised*—"positive" freedom—and must not be *violated*—"negative" freedom—the two kinds appearing as two perspectives of one and the same system of "rights." The harm principle is vacuous prior to a system of liberties and rights, while posterior to it all it does say is that the holders of liberties and rights are not to be deprived of them either by the state or by anybody else. Concisely, the harm principle affirms no more than that liberties are liberties and rights are rights.

The Kantian equal liberty, whether or not equipped with a maximizing clause, is baffling in its lack of guidance about what exactly is, or ought to be made, equal—and subject to equality, maximal. It appears, at first blush, to have to do with the distribution among individuals of something finite, quantifiable and variable, analogous to a stretch devoid of obstacles, a level surface, a private space, a protected sphere. If this were a possible interpretation and freedom were a quantifiable dimension—or dimensions—of states of affairs, it would make perfect sense to say that one person disposed of more of it than another—a test of equality—or could have more if another had less—a test that problems of distribution are technically soluble—and that if there were more of it altogether, at least some—and subject to solving problems of distribution, all—could have more, which may also mean that by giving some more of it, it can be maximized—a test that maximization is a practical objective. The difficulty is that the analogy between unobstructed length, surface or space, and freedom, is just that, an analogy and no more. There seems to be no apparent way in which freedom could be quantified. I suggest that the statement that two persons are "equally free" has the same cognitive status as that they are "equally happy" or "equally handsome"; these are statements of somebody's judgment from the evidence, but the same evidence could have induced somebody else to pass a different judgment and it is impossible conclusively to settle, from the evidence alone, which of two contradictory judgments is more nearly right. There is no agreed arbitrator, nor is a last-resort test built into the practice of these subjective comparisons for settling contrary judgments and perceptions. On the view that inter-personal comparisons of such states of mind conditions as utility, happiness or satisfaction are a category-mistake to begin with, and that the freedom of one person, being as it is bound up with subjective perceptions, is similarly incomparable to the freedom of another, the whole practice of seeking their levels or the extent of differences between them may be logically suspect anyway. In its normative version, "equal freedom" is no more stringent than Dworkin's "equal concern and respect," the central plank in his democratic ethics, rightly dismissed by Raz with the deadpan finding that it "seems to mean that everyone has a right to concern and respect."[12] Like "equal respect," the norm of "equal freedom" is unexceptionable, due in no small measure to its non-committal vagueness: practically *any* feasible state of affairs can be claimed, without fear of rebuttal, to be satisfying such norms.[13]

If it is reasonable to read the Marxist concept of freedom as emancipation from the regime of "reified relations" and mastery over one's material destiny, and then to translate this into less exalted English as the abolition of commodity and labor markets, the concept is extravagant but not vacuous. "Abolition of the market" and "resource allocation by the political authority" have sufficiently precise factual content that can be empirically recognized as being or not being the case. Unlike "arbitrary will," "minimum necessary coercion" or "equal liberty," they are ascertainable features of a given social state of affairs: they either obtain or they do not. A Ministry of Planning and Rationing cannot very well be "deconstructed" and shown to be "really" a market in thin disguise. Where Marxist freedom nevertheless convicts itself of vacuousness and moral truism is in tirelessly transforming and qualifying descriptive statements, till they cease to describe anything that is ascertainable. "Servitude" is not to the conditions of the market, but to its "blind caprice," its "irrationality"; absence of central resource allocation is a "chaotic, self-destructive" system; "the product is master of the producer"; "man, too, may be a commodity" and as such becomes "a plaything of chance."[14] Production under socialist planning is not in obedience to the instructions of the political authority—a testable statement—but "according to need"—an irrefutable vacuity. Any situation, whatever its characteristic empirical data, can be qualified as harmonious or a tooth-and-claw jungle war; any resource allocation can safely be called socially optimal or condemned as "bureaucratic," hence failing to produce "according to needs." There is the compulsion to agree to the moral truism that rational, conscious social deliberation is more conducive to the freedom of mankind than irrational, unconscious thrashing about in the dark; but as we can never tell which is which, the agreement is easy; freedom's name is taken in vain and does not commit anyone to anything.

The Freedom That Hurts

The rough underside of freedom is responsibility for oneself. The fewer the institutional obstacles an individual faces in choosing acts to fit his preferences, the more his life is what he makes it, and the less excuse he has for what he has made of it. The looser the man-made constraints upon him, the less he can count on others being constrained to spare his interests and help him in need. The corollary of an individual's discretion to contribute to or coldly ignore the purposes of the community is that he has no good claims upon it to advance his purposes. It may be that immunity from the "arbitrary will" of others is coextensive with freedom, but so is dependence on one's own talents, efforts and luck. As Toynbee put it, the "road from slavery to freedom is also the road from security to insecurity of maintenance."

The agreeable corollary of my right is the duty of others to respect it; less agreeably, *their* right entails *my* duty. Freedom, if it has ascertainable content, turns out to have attendant costs, and, if freedom has degrees, the greater it is, probably the higher is its opportunity cost. Trade-offs between freedom and other goods are manifest facts of social life, though it may be embarrassing to admit to our better selves how often we take advantage of them. By no means is it evident that men want all the freedom that tyrannical or "bureaucratic" political systems deny them.

The less nebulous and the more matter-of-fact is the content of freedom, the more obtrusive become its costs. Nowhere is this so clear as in the matter of the most contested safeguard of freely chosen individual action, that is private property. Freedom of contract, privacy and private property rights are mutually entailed. Complete respect for either member of the triad would exclude taxation. Even when it has no deliberate redistributive function, taxation simultaneously violates privacy, property rights and the freedom of contract as the taxpayer loses the faculty to dispose of part of his resources by voluntary contract, and must permit the political authority to dispose of it by command. A reconciliation between the freedom of contract—and by implication, private property and taxation—is offered by social contract theory, whose assumptions lead to taxation, as well as political obedience in general, being recognized as if it were voluntarily undertaken.

There is a tendency, cutting across the political spectrum from left to right, to see private property as divisible into several distinct and independent rights.[15] While this position is certainly tenable, its consequence is to encourage the view that restrictions on transfers of ownership, rent, dividend and price controls, the regulation of corporate control etc., are consistent with the integrity of private property. If the latter is to be regarded as a "bundle" consisting of a number of separable rights, any one of these measures leaves all other rights within the bundle inviolate; yet any one of them is a violation of the freedom of contract. No ambiguity about their mutual entailment arises when property is conceived as an integral, indivisible right.

Adherence to any maximizing principle of freedom[16] *prima facie* implies non-violation of the freedom of contract, for it would be extravagant to maintain that its restriction, whatever its purportedly beneficial effects on, say, efficiency or income distribution, somehow leaves intact, let alone contributes to maximize, freedom in general. Moreover, if freedom is really about the unobstructed faculty of every sane adult person to be the judge of his own interest, acting as he sees fit and "doing what he desires,"[17] freedom of contract must be its irreducible hard core. To argue in the same breath for maximized (and "equal") freedom in general and restricted freedom of contract, seems to me to presuppose that we judge *unilateral* and potentially "Pareto-inferior" acts not requiring the consent of a contracting party by a liberal standard, bilateral and presumably "Pareto-superior" ones, depending on willing reciprocity of two or more parties, by a more severe one. Yet this is surely applying the standards the wrong way round. If a double standard were admissible, and necessary to sort out actions that *should* from those that should *not* be interfered with, the easier one should be applied to contracts since, unlike unilateral acts, they have passed a prior test of mutual consent by the parties most directly concerned. The chosen action of one person that is not contingent on the agreed cooperation of another and may leave the latter worse off, can hardly have a better claim to the social *laissez passer* of freedom from legalized obstruction, than the proposed action that must, for its realization, first obtain the agreement and fit in with the matching proposed action of a potential contracting party.

Insistence on freedom of contract and on its corollaries, property and privacy, is a hard position that attracts only a minority constituency of doctrinaires on the one hand, old-fogey-nostalgics of a better past that never really was, on the other. Such a constituency is naturally suspect. Its stand offends the moral reflexes of a broad public; for it is yet another moral truism that fair prices, fair rents, fair wages and conditions of employment, fair trade, fair competition are incontrovertibly better and worthier of approval than prices, rents, wages, etc. that have merely been agreed in a bargain without being necessarily fair. Anyone who contests this may be putting an ulterior motive above justice, and the onus of proving the contrary is on him.

A somewhat more clever argument that does not directly beg the question of fairness holds that even if a bargain between willing parties at some point on their contract curve is "in itself" better than failing to agree and staying off the curve, some points are nevertheless better than others for one party, worse for the other. In two-person or two-group face-to-face dealings, the actual point they agree on is partly a matter of their relative bargaining power, which must in turn depend on the distribution of wealth, will, skill and so forth. Untrammelled freedom of contract subject only to no force and fraud thus gives "a moral blessing to the inequalities of wealth,"[18] and, for that matter, of abilities and other advantages. Commitment to it is a commitment *both* to a maximizing principle of freedom and to non-interference with a given distribution of natural and acquired assets.

An attempt to escape from this commitment, with which many feel ill at ease and vulnerable, is to promote the idea that there could be an initial distribution of advantages that would act as a "level playing field." Once this special distribution is achieved—by redistribution of acquired and transferable assets, such as wealth, and by compensatory measures of "positive discrimination" in education to offset natural and non-transferable advantages, such as talent and intelligence—freedom of contract becomes not only compatible with justice but is the very means to it. It produces "pure procedural justice," in the same way as a game played by the rules on a level playing field by definition produces a just result. This particular distribution-cum-compensatory-discrimination amounts to a state of equal opportunity for all. Under equality of opportunity, freedom of contract gives rise to outcomes that need not be overridden in the interest of justice. Equality of opportunity, freedom of contract and just outcomes, constitute a triadic relation such that any two entail the third. In terms of causation, the first two jointly constitute the procedure whose outcome is distributive justice.

This attempt at squaring freedom with justice must clear two hurdles, the first substantive, the second analytical. The substantive hurdle concerns the practical possibility of levelling the playing-field, instead of perversely making it more uneven in the attempt. I do not intend to discuss this problem (except to note that it is a genuine one), and could not resolve it if I did. The second hurdle consists in the argument for procedural justice proving to depend on self-contradictory reasoning. A distribution of resources and advantages is both an end-state, and a starting position leading to a new distribution. The object of a particular initial distribution D, offering equal opportunities, is to have the freedom of contract to produce just outcomes. However, whatever outcome D' it did produce will differ from the initial equal-opportunity distribution D; some people will have gotten ahead of the position—in terms of wealth, skills, reputation, place in the social network—assigned to them in the equal-opportunity distribution, others will have lagged behind it. (Countless handicap races have been run on the world's race courses but despite the best efforts of expert handicappers, there is to my knowledge no record of a single race ever producing a dead heat of *all* the runners). We need not decide whether this is an empirical law or a logical necessity. Such will be the just outcome of the first round; however, this just end-state represents a new distribution D' of assets and advantages that, unlike the initial D, no longer offers equal opportunities for the second round. Equality of opportunity must be restored by redistribution, positive discrimination and so forth. The just end-state D' generated by equal opportunities and freedom of contract in the first round offers the participants unequal opportunities for the second round, and must be overridden to secure the justice of the end-state to be generated in it, and so on to the third and all subsequent rounds to the end of time.

The contradiction in the reasoning of many liberals who want to embrace a plurality of values, seek the reconciliation of freedom and justice, and find in equality of opportunity combined with freedom of contract the joint necessary and sufficient conditions of a procedural type of social justice, resides in this: 1) a particular end-state distribution D, and only D, is consistent with equality of opportunity, 2) equality of opportunity combined with freedom of contract engenders non-D, and only non-D, 3) D is not compatible with procedural distributive justice, 4) therefore equality of opportunity, freedom of contract and procedural distributive justice are not mutually compatible.

The reader will remark that if equality of opportunity is not itself a final value, but has only instrumental value in bringing about a certain valuable end-state, yet that kind of end-state must continually be overridden because it is inconsistent with the maintenance of equality of opportunity, the instrumental value of the latter is fleeting and self-destructive. If it is to be commended, it must be on its own merits as a final value, and not for its instrumental capacity to bring about procedural justice in distribution. If no equivalent procedure suggests itself, the attempt at procedural distributive justice must be considered a failure, the justice or otherwise of a distribution must be ascertained in some other manner, such as by listening to the moral consensus of public opinion, and the just distribution either given up as too costly and awkward to achieve, or enforced by direct measures that *ipso facto* violate the freedom of contract and the corollary rights of property and privacy.

Twist it as we may, the dilemma will not go away. The hard sort of freedom that is more than moral truism and non-committal, costless piety, forbids the exercise of social choice over questions of "who gets what." Yet that is the crucial domain over which voters, groups, classes and their coalitions generally aspire, and often succeed, to turn the power of the political authority to their advantage. More freedom is less scope for collective choice and vice versa; there is a trade-off which democratic society has used these past hundred years or so to whittle down freedom sometimes overtly, sometimes surreptitiously and the most often fairly unconsciously. The process of whittling down has been promoted and justified by a more plausible and seductive ideology than anything classical liberals could muster.

No Hard Choices

The ideology of the expanding domain of social choice used to have, and probably has not lost, the ambition of showing how this is compatible with the avoidance of hard choices, notably the preservation of freedom. Two key theses serve as its twin pillars.

The first, put briefly, concerns the reliance on reason. It seems to affirm that, whether embodied in the knowledge of a technocratic elite or in the consensual wisdom born of democratic debate, reason is the only guide we should follow, and, in a more exacting and activist version, we should never fail to follow. Reason is in most circumstances able to detect faults in the functioning of economic and social arrangements, and can prescribe the likely remedy. This thesis is common to doctrines as disparate as Benthamite utilitarianism, Saint Simonian, Marxist or just *ad hoc* socialism, Fabian compromise, "constructivist" system-building and Popperite trial-and-error social engineering. They are consequentialist doctrines, willing the means if they will the end: they fear no taboos and stop at no barriers of a non-reasoned and metaphysical nature.

All hold, albeit implicitly, that government whose vocation it is to elicit and execute social choices, is a uniquely potent tool which it is wasteful and inefficient not to employ to capacity for bringing about feasible improvements. Government, and it alone, can correct the deformities of markets. It can deal with unwanted externalities and regulate the conduct of private enterprise when the divergence of private and social costs and returns misguides it by false signals. Forgoing society's political power to improve results in these respects, and indeed in any others, is irrational and obscurantist.

Without actually being a series of truisms, the easy plausibility of this thesis makes it near-invincible in public debate. Counter-arguments, if directed against "excessive interference" and "bureaucratic busybodyness," are irrefutable but ineffective, since meliorist measures dictated by reason are never *meant* to be excessive or bureaucratic. A general plea to leave well alone is, to all intents and purposes, a defeatist or uncaring stance against trying to do better. Each policy, each measure is defended piecemeal by reason, on its separate merits. The perhaps unintended sum of winning piecemeal arguments for doing this and that, is a win for government intervention as a general practice. The twin of the thesis about reason is about justice. The former aims at allocative efficiency, the latter at the right distribution of the product. The dual structure of the domain of social choice suggested by this division of aims, implies that logically and temporally production comes first, distribution follows second. Things are produced, as Mill believed, according to "the laws of economics," and once they are there, become available for distribution according to some other law or precept. Such has been the position of Christian Socialists since high medieval times, and such is that of redistributor liberals from Mill and T.H. Green to Rawls. Distributions caused by the hazard of heredity, heritage and history may be freely altered, subject only to limits set by expediency, by social choice which is sovereign over the matter. They ought to be altered, to conform to some moral standard, because they are morally arbitrary.

The charge of moral arbitrariness, if it is upheld, means no more than it says, namely that rewards are not, or not wholly, determined by the moral features of a social state of affairs: the morally arbitrary distribution fails to fulfill the positive prediction that people's incomes, etc. depend on their deserts, as well as the normative postulate that they ought to depend on them. However, a cognitive diagnosis of arbitrariness might be applied to a distribution not only from the moral, but also from the economic, legal, social or historical points of view. A morally arbitrary distribution fails to conform to a moral theory; arbitrariness, however, may also obtain with respect to economic, legal or historical theories of distribution as well. If the actual distribution is partly determined by genetic endowments and their development, character, education, wealth and chance, which seems to me a sensible hypothesis, it has, from the point of view of any theory which does not properly account for these factors, an ineradicable property of un-caused randomness, or to use the value-loaded synonym, "arbitrariness." Thus, we can say that, in terms of the marginal productivity theory of factor rewards, the distribution of factor incomes in the Soviet Union is arbitrary. That, however, does not in itself condemn it. Arbitrariness is an obstacle to explaining or predicting, and it is also the absence of reasons for upholding or commending a particular distribution, but it is not a reason for changing it.[19] Some further, positive argument is needed to make the case that an arbitrary distribution ought to be purged of its random features and transformed into one that fully obeys some ordering principle drawn from a moral (or some other) theory.

It would be too easy if the ideology which, for its completeness, needed a theory of distributive justice, could validate the latter by the mere claim, however well founded, that the actual distribution was arbitrary. The theory needs the support of axioms that must be independent, difficult to reject and adequate. However, what axioms will bear the weight of a theory that must justify the subjection of who-gets-what questions to the political authority? Neither moral desert[20] nor the various versions of egalitarianism are difficult enough to reject.

Moral desert lacks independence, in that what is judged as morally deserved, obviously depends on an (at least implicit) moral theory guiding such judgments. Only prior agreement on such a theory, and notably on its implications for distributive justice, can secure agreed judgments of moral desert. They are indeterminate without the support of the theory, hence cannot serve as its antecedents.

Unlike moral desert, egalitarianism is at least not circular, and can be, though it rarely is, non-vacuous, i.e. its necessary conditions can be so defined that whether they are fulfilled or not becomes an empirical question. However, little else is left to be said for it. As an instrumental value, it used to be bolstered by consequentialist arguments, e.g. maximization of utility from a given total income, better satisfaction of "real needs" or reduced pain of envy, that no longer enjoy much intellectual credit. As an ultimate, non-instrumental value that need not be argued for, it retains the emotional appeal it always had and probably always will have; paradoxically, however, the clearer it becomes that the appeal is essentially emotional, the more its effect fades.

On the whole, like certain seductive mining prospects that have been sadly spoiled by the drilling of core samples, distributive justice loses some of its glitter in analysis. "A distribution ought to be just" is a plausible requirement. "A just distribution ought to correspond to moral deserts," or "a just distribution ought to be equal" are a good deal easier to contradict. Moreover, attempts to put such norms into practice have not helped either, ranging as they did from the disappointing when they were ineffective, to the disastrous when they were effective. Sir Stafford Cripps, Olaf Palme and Willy Brandt have done much to make redistributive compromises unappealing. Pol Pot and Nicolae Ceauscescu have done as much for the uncompromising variety.

A more ingenious strategy proceeds by revising the order of the arguments. The usual sequence is to propose that, 1) the existing distribution is arbitrary, 2) only non-arbitrary distributions can be just, 3) a just distribution conforms to an appropriate ordering principle, 4) social choice legitimately mandates the government to realize this conformity. Instead of this roundabout route to the sovereignty of social choice over distribution, it is more efficient directly to propose that the assets, endowments and other advantages that make the existing distribution what it is, are not rightfully owned by the persons to whom they are in various ways attached, but are the property of their community,[21] and it is up to the community to decide the disposal of the fruits of its property. Genetic qualities, wealth, acquired knowledge and organization all belong to society as a whole and are *eo ipso* subject to social choice, without any need for a legitimation drawn from controversial requirements of justice, and a debatable mandate for actually imposing them.

Distributions "chosen by society" may or may not be just. They are *ipso facto* just only in case the moral axioms that are used to define the justice or otherwise of a distribution, are taken to be the same as those that help, by fixing the choice rule, to identify an alternative as the "socially chosen" one. This means, broadly speaking, that if in a given political society the "chosen" alternative is some resultant of the wishes of its members, if every member's wish "counts for one and no more than one," and the majority wish prevails, then the "just" distribution is identified by the same rule in the same way. "Just" then means "chosen by society," found to be such by a democratic process of search and consultation, or, more loosely, conforming to the moral consensus. It is just that a person should be allowed to keep what he has if, and only if, more people than not think that he should. This is perhaps a brutal and unsympathetic statement of what the sovereignty of social choice implies, but it is by no means a caricature of it.

The real difference between the two ideological strategies for extending the domain of social choice consists in this: if assets, in the broad sense which includes wealth, skill and character, belong to individuals in a "capitalist free-for-all," there is a *prima facie* implication that it is their right to dispose of the resulting income, both "earned" and "unearned." Society, however, speaking by the medium of the "social choice rule" might declare such an income distribution unjust, refuse to countenance it and proceed to its redistribution. In doing so, it would contradict itself, for it could not in the same breath both respect and violate a given set of property rights with the attendant freedom of contract. Its solution, adopted, as Hayek called them in the *Road to Serfdom*, by "socialists of all parties" except the genuine ones, is to chop up property rights into a variety of separate rights, recognize and attach some to certain classes of asset or asset-holder, and detach others, depending on the origin, type or size of the asset or advantage in question, finally declaring its unshaken respect for the resulting mishmash. Ownership of property and the right to use, sell, bequeath, rent or consume it thus become disjointed, fitting together as *ad hoc* "social choices" decree. In conjunction with this solution, society or its government can affirm allegiance to any innocuous notion of freedom, and for good measure even give it "lexicographic priority," that requires the non-violation of rights in general without committing itself to specific and potentially inconvenient rights, and to the freedom of contract in particular.

Genuine socialists, probably no longer a very numerous or happy class, face no such contradiction between private rights and the ambition for social choice to override them, and need not have recourse to the ambiguities of redistributor liberals. With property vested in society, it is "social choice" that by rights distributes incomes, positions and ranks in the first place; it does not need to redistribute what it has distributed, hence it does not come into conflict with any right it may have recognized to begin with; the problem of the freedom of contract does not even arise.

One way or the other, as long as freedom is allowed to be "soft," nebulous, innocuous, costless, and as long as the claim that it is being respected and its conditions are fulfilled, remains "unfalsifiable" because the conditions are vacuous and commit to little, there are no hard choices. Allocative efficiency and social justice can be pursued in conjunction with the "greatest possible" and most "equal" freedom. We can have it all. By contrast, the painful trade-offs imposed by laying down "hard," specific, falsifiable conditions of freedom can be made to stand out clearly. Privacy, private property and freedom of contract strike at the heart of "social choice," removing as they do from its domain many of the most valuable opportunities any decisive subset of society would use for imposing on the superset the choices and solutions it prefers, considers right or just, or expects to profit from.

Non-violation of privacy, private property and freedom of contract involves massive self-denial. It demands a large measure of renunciation of the use of political processes for advancing certain interests in conflict with others. Instead of getting their way, majorities may have to bargain and buy it by contractual means. It also involves negation of plausible and well-developed ideologies that would justify the use of political power to promote one's selfish or unselfish ends in the name of allocative efficiency or social justice.[22] Small wonder, then, that these principles of freedom are systematically violated or talked out of existence. The contrary would be surprising in a civilization with a good deal of political sophistication, skills of adversarial argument and no inconvenient taboos; a civilization like our own.

THE BITTER MEDICINE OF FREEDOM

Undeserved Luck

The problem is not how to explain why enlightened men do not noticeably like the more-than-rhetorical freedom that imposes upon them self-denial, renunciation, responsibility and duty. It is to account for the far stranger fact that, perhaps for the first time in a hundred-odd years, this freedom most of us do not really like is nevertheless holding its own. It seems actually to have gained in some important countries of the political West, and has ceased to retreat in most others. From an abysmal starting level, it is clearly in the ascendant in the societies of the political "East," that had set out really to build socialism and have found that they have inadvertently joined the Third World in the process. Why should the relentless expansion of the domain of collective choice, which has all the logic of political power behind it, now be checked and reversed in so many different places?

Each of these societies has its particular case history; each is no doubt rich in particular lessons. This is not the occasion to survey their more bizarre episodes and their high and low moments. As always, however, each case history has much in common with every other. The chief common feature, to my mind, is that the cumulative imposition by "social choice" of reasoned solutions to an infinity of problems in production and distribution, efficiency and justice, has gradually built up perverse effects, whose total weight finally sufficed to convert the afflicted society to the bitter medicine of freedom.

It is important to admit and indeed to underline that the attempted solutions were reasoned. The caprice of the tyrant played little part in modern attempts at social problem-solving. In each instance, some sort of rational case could be constructed for them. Nothing is easier than to state with hindsight that the case for solution A was "obviously" false and owed its adoption to the stupidity or wickedness of politicians. Nothing is more dangerous than to follow up this train of thought with the all too frequent suggestion that because A was so obviously wrong, B ought to have been chosen. This is

53

the sort of argument that would always justify one more try[23] and would give rise to an endless chain of measures, instead of to the decisive abandonment of tinkering. Often we reason as if alternative measures and policies came with labels describing the likely effects of each, and perhaps also the "objective" probability that a particular effect will manifest itself. If this were so, the social choice of policies would be a choice between sets of specified consequences, or their probability distributions. Better policies would therefore on the whole tend to be chosen in preference to worse ones. Logically the power of the political authority to put chosen policies into practice would be beneficial at least in the long run, over large numbers of measures; collective choice equipped with such coercive power would have a good chance of yielding better results than the sum of individual choices that has lacked such power; and the enlargement of the collective domain at the expense of "hard" freedom would augment the scope for better results. Power, chance and scope would jointly work for progress, and speed us towards the meliorist ideal.

In reality, the labels the policies carry specify only the narrow band of their effects that have reasonably good visibility. Only hindsight shows that there always is, in addition, a broader and fuzzier band of consequences whose *ex ante* predictability must have been very low, very conjectural or simply non-existent. Whether this is so because our knowledge about these matters is inadequate though capable of improvement, or because they are inherently unknowable, is perhaps immaterial at any period in time for the consequentialist evaluation of a policy. There may, in addition, be effects that are reasonably predictable but so slow to mature that they get heavily discounted at the inception of a measure—discounting, of course, is a legitimate and indeed a mandatory operation in the rational calculus—and only begin seriously to hurt when the measure that has caused them is as good as forgotten together with the men who had chosen it.

THE BITTER MEDICINE OF FREEDOM

I propose to call unwelcome consequences "perverse" in a broad sense, not only when they are the direct opposite of the main aim of a policy (e.g., a redistributive measure intended to decrease inequality which in fact increases it; a policy of import substitution which makes exports shrink more than imports; government sponsorship of research that actually retards technological progress, and so forth) but also when, acting over a more diffuse area, indirectly or in unexpected directions, they impose costs and reduce benefits so as to leave society worse off than if a given policy had not been adopted. I am aware that condemning a measure on this ground may be question-begging for two reasons. First, the imputation to it of particular unwelcome effects may be too conjectural when the supposed causation is indirect. It may be that lavish spending on arms over the last decade has for roundabout reasons weakened the war making ability and fighting prowess of both the great powers, but how can the diagnosis of cause and effect be made conclusive? Second, a judgment that society is on balance worse off when certain things, say inflation or child delinquency, have gone wrong but others, say care for the old or water pollution, have gone right, is forever fated to depend on how homogenous weights are to be assigned to heterogenous variables; give greater weight to the ones which have gone right, and you find society better off.

Nevertheless, there are well within our memory unmitigated disasters, utter failures and glaring disproportions between outlay and return, where a distinct policy is so clearly the prime suspect in producing perverse effects that it is bad faith or intellectual preciosity to argue the incompleteness of the proof. The collectivization of land and the attendant pursuit of "economies of scale" in agriculture and, for that matter, in manufacturing too, is now almost unanimously recognized as an act of self-mutilation that has done irreparable damage to the Soviet Union. Strengthening the powers, disciplinary cohesion and legal immunities of trade unions, and taking them into the corporatist conspiracy of the Macmillan, Wilson and Heath years is now, albeit less unanimously, seen as a major cause of the "English disease." The policy of forcibly diverting investment from the rest of Italy to its Mezzogiorno has not only cost the country dear in direct and indirect ways—that transferring benefits from one part of society to another is not costless is after all quite consistent with the fond supposition that the exercise nevertheless has a "positive sum"—but may not even have been of real net benefit to the Mezzogiorno.

There are less localized examples of once respected policies that are now highly suspect of perverse effects. Progressive taxation is one: even its natural advocates have learnt to say that it must not be "too" progressive. Free, universal, non-selective formal education, no "streaming," no elitism, diplomas for all, open access for all to universities crowned by the principle of one man-one Ph.D., is another. We are discovering that it hinders the education of those who could profit from it and wastes the time of the rest, breeds student unrest and disappointment, and buys these personal and social blessings at a near-crippling cost to the community's finances. Public policies of welfare and public guarantees (including compulsory insurance) against risks and wants of various kinds in both "mixed" and avowedly "socialist" economies, are coming to be suspected of generating unwelcome behavioral changes: sluggishness to respond to incentives and opportunities, poor resistance to adverse conditions, a weakening of the "work ethic," free riding, irresponsibility for oneself and one's offspring, a falling personal propensity to save, over-consumption and waste of freely provided public goods; these costs, and the long-run damage they do to society's capacity to function, and to the character and virtue of its members, are beginning to weigh heavily against the putative gain in welfare and social justice of which they are dimly perceived to be a by-product.

Not that disillusion, suspicion and an "agonizing reappraisal" of their costs and benefits is actually leading to the wholesale rolling back of these policies. But their easy expansion has by and large been checked, and in some areas collective choice seems to be restraining itself to give way to the operation of "hard," non-vacuous freedom principles. Its remaining champions, by way of last-ditch defense, design fallback positions holding out the same old promise that we can, after all, have it both ways. Though they have mostly given up talk about the Yugoslav Road, the Third Way, Indicative Planning and Social Justice In a Free Society, and though such magic passwords to coercion as "prisoners' dilemma," "externality" and "community preference ordering" may with luck soon go the way of "the diminishing marginal utility of money" and "pump-priming for full employment," the intellectual advocacy of using the power of collective decisions to make a better world will never cease. There are still so many good ideas left! Assuredly, we have not heard the last of the prize inanity, market socialism.

When and where societies, and the decision-making coalitions of interests within them, renounce to use their force for allocating resources and rewards, and take the bitter medicine of freedom instead, they do so because their meliorist solutions that would violate freedom, are proving too costly in perverse effects. Contrast this with the diametrically opposite position of actually liking freedom, even if it proved costly in material sacrifice. As Roepke[24] has movingly put it:

> I would stand for a free economic order even
> if it implied material sacrifice and if socialism
> gave the certain prospect of material increase.
> It is our undeserved luck that the exact oppo-
> site is true.

It is undeserved luck indeed. Where would we be now if socialism were affordable and whittling freedom down were not as expensive as we are finding it to be?

NOTES

1. F.H. Knight, 1943, 75.
2. F.A. Hayek, 1960, 11, 21.
3. Hayek, *op. cit.*, 11.
4. Cf. the 1791 *Declaration of the Rights of Man*; also J.S. Mill, 1848, Ch. 2.
5. "The most extensive basic liberty compatible with a similar liberty for others," Rawls, 1972, 60. Liberty, then, is to be increased as long as its further increase does not require some to have less of it than others; equality of freedom is a constraint on its maximization. This is implicit in the formula but is not spelt out by Rawls.
6. Hayek, *op. cit.*, 13.
7. Marx, 1843, 1975, 229.
8. Marx, 1844, 1975, *passim.*
9. More precisely, the species, the *Gattungswesen.*
10. Whether there is any satisfactory doctrine of necessary coercion is a vast open question, which I have tried to address at length elsewhere. Hayek, at all events, has not provided one; the coercion he considers justified because necessary to raise the means for providing useful public goods and services, including a social "safety net," is completely open-ended. It excludes as unnecessary the coercion involved in raising the means for useless public goods and services, or those that, though useful, could better be provided by private enterprise. This leaves a quasi-infinity of occasions for necessary coercion, or at least for coercion that can never be proven unnecessary by the loose Hayek criteria.
11. Cf., however, the approach adopted by Feinberg, 1984.
12. Raz, 1986, 220.
13. One of Rawls's two versions of equal liberty, that consisting of an integrated, coherent "system...defining rights and duties" (*op. cit.*, 202) seems to me clearly open to this charge. In the other version, the system is said to consist

of a number of distinct "basic liberties" (*op. cit.*, 302) of "equal citizenship." They are the conventional political freedoms ensuring democratic representation and equality before the law, and they are not vacuous. They seem to me, however, too confined in their effects and therefore inadequate to pass for a "principle of liberty." For one, they offer too few safeguards to minorities against the will of the majority. For another, they provide no defense of property, nor of privacy. Such "basic liberties" leave the respective domains of individual and collective choice wholly indeterminate.

14. F. Engels, 1891, 1968, 680-1.
15. Cf. Alchian and Demsetz, 1973, 18.
16. "...an equal right to the most extensive total system of equal basic liberties"; Rawls, *op. cit.*, 302.
17. J.S. Mill, 1848, Ch. 5.
18. Atiyah, 1979, 337.
19. For a different argument about moral arbitrariness, cf. Nozick, 1974, 213-26.
20. There can, in any case, be no differential moral desert if all differential performance is due to some differential advantage (talent, education, character etc.), and all such advantages are themselves undeserved. Cf. Sandels, 1982, 88. Moral desert then collapses into equality, and becomes redundant.
21. G.A. Cohen in Paul, Miller, Paul and Ahrens, 1986.
22. Since "talk is cheap" and language will adapt to anything, one can override principles of freedom to advance one's interest in the name of freedom. When in 1776, in one of the failed attempts of the century to make French society more efficient and mobile, Turgot tried to put through a program of fairly extensive deregulation, the "duly constituted" corporations defended and saved regulation as a system of "real freedom," necessary for the public good.
23. In a large flock of geese, the most precious ones started to languish and die one by one. The wise rabbi was asked

to find a remedy. As each of his suggestions was put into practice, more geese died. When the wretched gooseherd finally reported the demise of his last bird, the rabbi, much annoyed, exclaimed: "What a shame, I had so many good ideas left!"

24. Roepke, 1959, 232.

WORKS CITED

A. Alchian and H. Demsetz, "The Property Rights Paradigm," *Journal of Economic History*, 1973, Vol. 33.

P.S. Atiyah, *The Rise and Fall of the Freedom of Contract*, 1979.

F. Engels, "The Origin of the Family, Private Property and the State," 1891, in Marx and Engels, *Selected Writings*, 1968.

J. Feinberg, *Harm to Others*, 1984.

F.A. Hayek, *The Constitution of Liberty*, 1960.

F.H. Knight, "The Meaning of Freedom," in C.H. Perry, ed. *The Philosophy of American Democracy*, 1943.

K. Marx, "The Jewish Question," 1843, Economic and Philosophical Manuscripts, 1844, in *Early Writings*, 1975.

J.S. Mill, *Principles of Political Economy*, 1848.

R. Nozick, *Anarchy, State, Utopia*, 1974.

E.F. Paul, F.D. Miller Jr., J. Paul and J. Ahrens, eds., *Marxism and Liberalism*, 1986.

J. Rawls, *A Theory of Justice*, 1972.

J. Raz, *The Morality of Freedom*, 1986.

W. Roepke, "The Economic Necessity of Freedom," *Modern Age*, 1959, reprinted with a foreword by E.J. Feulner, Jr., The Heritage Foundation, 1988.

M.J. Sandels, *Liberalism and The Limits of Justice*, 1982.

THREE

EQUALITY AND THE RULE OF LAW

George P. Fletcher

Everyone seems to agree that the rule of law is an indispens-able feature of modern political life. Whether one speaks of *regle de droit, Rechtsstaat,* or in the phrase that Gorbachev coined *provovoe gosudarsivo* [state based on law], government by law is, next to democracy, the popular demand of our times. In the extraordinary struggle for democracy everywhere from Eastern Europe to Western Asia, the "rule of law" comes readily to the lips of the reformers.

Where liberty asserts itself, the demand for the law will not be far behind. But what does this "rule of law" amount to? The extreme alternatives seem fairly clear: arbitrary rule by bureaucrats, terror from above, a cult of personal leadership; but, once rid of these infelicitous prospects, it is not clear what we should demand under the banner of the "rule of law" as it is expressed in English or in any of its analogues in European languages.

In this chapter I want to explore two themes in the ongoing discussion about what it means to be governed by law rather than to be subject to arbitrary orders and decrees. The first theme is the notion of being governed by rules. What does it mean for legal language to constrain the decisions of a judge?

THE BALANCE OF FREEDOM

It is possible, given the vicissitudes of disputes, for a set of rules to exhaust and control judicial decisions and to render the judges, in the words of Montesquieu, *la bouche de la loi* [a mouth of the law].

The second theme is whether, if governance by rules is possible, something more—something in the nature of the value of commitments—is necessary to realize what democratic reformers have in mind when they raise the banner of the rule of law. In particular, I am concerned about the connection between equality and the rule of law.

I. Governance by Rules

The starting place of our inquiry is the widespread view that the rule of law amounts to the law of rules. The picture seems to be that of decision makers bound by a rule book that tells them what to do in every conceivable case. The legal system is then complete and decisive in every case. Judges function as the medium but not the creative source of the decision. In the phrase coined by Brendan Sullivan, judges spout decisions as "potted plants" grow leaves. Lawyers have often dubbed this view of the legal process as "mechanical" or "slot machine justice."

So far as I know, no one trained in the law has ever taken this vision of a complete and decisive legal system seriously. The problems of life are too various, and our language too vague, to hope to conquer life with the language of rules. It seems to be almost a matter of lawyerly creed these days that modernity brings forth unforeseen problems; therefore, there is no way to anticipate all possible issues with a set of enacted laws.

The only serious example of a total and complete legal system is the Talmud, a compendium of discussions and solutions to concrete problems, both real and hypothetical, that purports to cover the terrain of human experience. Learned, religious Jews seek to live out their days by the instructions implicit in the Talmudic discussion. But note that the ideal conveyed in the Talmud is not that of a judge acting

62

as *la bouche de la loi,* but rather the ideal of the anarchist. In a total legal system, like that envisioned by the Talmud, judges are superfluous—at least so far as the law goes. If the system is total and complete, umpires must judge the facts, but no official need interpret and apply the law. No agents of the government need enforce the law. Every citizen is capable of knowing the law and applying it to the facts of his or her life experience. The life of Talmud-oriented Jews does not realize this ideal, but the aspiration of a self-administering legal system may once have been a factor motivating devotion of Talmudic studies.

No modern legal system has ever purported to take this ideal of a self-administering system as its goal. Even the modern European legal systems, based supposedly on codification, recognize the indispensable role of scholars and ever more of courts in concretizing the general legislative norms for application in particular cases. Neither statutes governing specific problems nor systemized codes strive to be exhaustive.

The central question in the legal thought of this century has been to develop an adequate theory of the relationship of legal language to the concrete decisions of judges. The two extreme positions are easy to state and equally easy to dismiss as unacceptable. At one extreme is the plain man's view of judges as "the mouth of the law," and at the opposite extreme is the so-called "realist" view, advocated by Jerome Frank and Karl Llewellyn in the 1940s and 1950s, that the law is nothing more than judges expressing their own political views in particular cases. Another way to put these two extremes is that according to the former view, the judge as person, as individual, contributes nothing to the decisions he or she reaches; the decisions follow logically, as it were, from the law. According to the latter view, the creative impulses of the judge generates the decision, and the law itself contributes nothing.

Both of these extreme views are naive. Neither accounts for the phenomenology of judging cases under law. Neither accounts adequately for the experience of living in a legal system, cognizant, in some complicated way, that both the language of the law and the personality of the judge flow into the decisions of the courts. The problem that legal theory has not adequately resolved is how precisely these two factors—the law itself and the personal value commitments of the judge—interweave in generating judicial decisions.

There are two basic strategies in the literature for coping with the extreme claim that all legal decisions are but political acts in disguise. One strategy stresses the controlling effect of legal language, and the alternative, the implication of the judge's duty to find the right answer to the dispute. The first of these approaches is associated with the name of H.L.A. Hart; the second, most significantly, with Ronald Dworkin.

When Hart wrote his classic, *The Concept of Law*, in 1961, the prevailing theory was the realist view that the law was indeterminate, that judges decided cases on the basis of their personal preferences. Carefully analyzing the notion of rules and the relationship of rules to decisions, Hart concluded that in at least the core or standard cases of a rule's application, the judge did not exercise any personal choice at all. The example that he made famous was a city ordinance prohibiting the introduction of vehicles into the city park. In the routine case, this rule carries a clear message: Do not drive your car or ride your bicycle in the park. But there are offbeat cases where the term vehicle appears to be equivocal and we are not sure whether the prohibition applies or not. If the Veterans Association wishes to mount a tank on a pedestal as a war memorial, we are simply not sure whether this constitutes a violation of the statute. In this borderline area of the rule, where the language offers no clear guidance, judges must intervene, Hart concedes, with a human component of "choice" or "discretion."

Hart's distinction between the core application of the rule and borderline or "penumbral" cases corresponds to lawyers' familiar distinction between easy cases and hard cases. In the easy case, the rule determines the outcome, precisely as the rule "three strikes, you're out" determines the status of a batter who has swung at and missed three pitches. In the hard case, the language of the rule is equivocal—as if a strike were defined as "pitch within a reasonable distance of home plate"—and the judge must fashion a decision, seemingly, by adding his personal judgments of fairness and sound policy.

For a graphic example from the current case law of the Supreme Court, think of the problem of determining whether communicable diseases, such as tuberculosis and AIDS, are to be treated as "handicaps" under the Federal Rehabilitation Act of 1973, which prohibits excluding from federally financed programs any "otherwise qualified handicapped individual."[1] Whether blind and crippled people are "handicapped" under the statute poses an easy case, but whether a person afflicted with contagious tuberculosis should be so treated is not so easily decided. In *School Board of Nassau County v. Arline,*[2] the Supreme Court confronted the question whether a school board in Florida could dismiss a teacher infected with contagious tuberculosis. The question holds great significance for the unresolved question whether persons with AIDS should receive the protection of the antidiscrimination statute.

The plain language of the statute hardly settles the matter. Not every person stricken with disease is "handicapped" in the ordinary meaning of the term. The legislative history of the statute fails to mention diseases as examples of the problem about which Congress was concerned. But the regulations interpreting the statute refer to "physiological disorder or condition" as the basis of handicaps, and this phrase arguably includes diseases like tuberculosis.

In the face of this ambiguity, how should the Supreme Court judges decide whether tuberculosis qualifies as a handicap? According to Hart's view, the case arises in the borderline area of the law and therefore the judges should exercise their "discretion" or make a "choice" in resolving the case. It is almost as though as soon as one passes from the realm of the easy to the hard case, one falls off the plateau of the law into an abyss of political and legislative choices. There must be a better way to conceptualize the relationship of hard to easy cases.

THE BALANCE OF FREEDOM

Dworkin responded to Hart's model of decision making by challenging whether judges ever exercise discretion or make a political choice in the same sense that legislators do.[3] The implication is that there is no significant difference between deciding whether blindness is a handicap and whether AIDS is a handicap. In both cases, Dworkin would argue, the judge is obligated to find the right answer to the problem. Implicitly, there is a truth of the matter and if so, the duty to determine the truth displaces the judges' discretion and freedom of choice. Judges have no more discretion in interpreting the meaning of "handicap" under the federal statute than historians have in seeking to grasp the truth about the past.

One way to seek the true meaning of "handicap" as the term is used in the statute is to construct a theory about the purpose and function of an ideal statute prohibiting discrimination against handicapped persons. It seems that the seven-person majority of the Court did just that in concluding that contagious tuberculosis was a handicap. The argument was that the "basic purpose of [the statute] was to ensure that handicapped individuals are not denied jobs or other benefits because of the prejudiced attitudes or the ignorance of others."[4] Because, the seven justices reasoned, the contagiousness of a disease like tuberculosis often generates a prejudiced response, a contagious disease that impairs a "major life activity"[5] can be considered a handicap.[6]

On the assumption that judges should adopt the theory of a statute that best makes sense of its language, the judges would have no discretion in deciding whether to adopt this theory—if it were indeed the best theory of the statute's purpose. Whether it is the best theory, however, is questionable. The court's construction seems to suffer the fallacy of confusing necessary and sufficient conditions for treating a condition as a handicap. It may be a necessary condition of handicapped persons that they are likely to generate prejudiced social response based on ignorance, but it does not follow that this reaction is sufficient to treat, for example, hair dyed purple as a handicap.

The two vote dissent in the *Arline* case responded to the majority's theory of the legislative purpose by accusing them of relying on their "own sense of fairness."[7] This was a covert way of suggesting that the court was in fact exercising its discretion and making a value choice rather than relying on the correct standard of decision.[8] That two justices dissented does not by itself prove that the majority did not have the best theory of the statute and resolved the case incorrectly, but the very fact of disagreement renders claims of truth more difficult to accept.

For the theory of judicial decision-making, the important point is not whether any particular court in fact gets the matter right, but whether one believes that in fact there is a truth of the matter, whether the right answer to the question, is tuberculosis a handicap?, can possibly be found. If the right answer exists, then it makes sense to impose a duty on judges to find that answer. And if judges are under that duty, then they no longer have discretion, the power to make a choice based on their personal "sense of fairness," in shaping the resolution of the dispute.

To review the two distinct approaches to the problem of judicial choice, the Hartian approach divides the ranges of possible cases into two: those wherein the language of the rule determines the outcome and those wherein it does not. The Dworkinian approach, as I am interpreting it,[9] shifts the focus of the inquiry from the controlling effect of language to the duty of judges to find the right answer, thereby implicitly assuming that a right answer exists. This answer, it must be noted, need not be found in the written materials of the law, but must be sought as well in general principles and values that inhere in the legal system. The difference between these two approaches derives, in part, from the initial ontological question: Does the right answer exist or does it not? If you say no, then you are inclined to think that the rule of law can be obtained only in the controlling effect of precisely worded legal rules. If you say yes, then you might be inclined to see judges not as mediators of disputes, but investigators committed to the truth.

We have identified, then, three distinct ways of thinking about the rule of law. To take the last variation first, "believers" have found a new champion in Ernest Weinrib, who wrote an eloquent defense of the "immanent moral rationality" of law.[12] In the same volume, Fred Schauer defends the "pragmatic-agnostic" version of the rule of law against the nihilists.[13]

At various times, in my own work, I have defended both versions of the formalistic school. I agree with Weinrib that the immanent purpose of litigation is to do corrective justice, rather than to achieve social justice through the systematic redistribution of wealth. The commitment to corrective justice yields certain consequences, such as the impermissibility of judging private disputes on the basis of the best interests of the society as a whole. Judges ought to focus on the dispute between the parties and not on the impact of their decisions on parties not before the court. Yet the most that one can get from this analysis is a view about the proper perspective of judges at the time of decision. Their focus should zero in on some considerations and not others. It is a long leap of faith, however, from a theory of focus to a commitment to there being a right answer in every case.

The pragmatic-agnostic version of formalism obviously has merit, but I think this line of theorists, from Hart to Schauer, has made a fundamental mistake in stressing the controlling effect of legal language per se. Legal language apart from context has no effect whatsoever. Schauer seems to think that statutory prohibitions are contextual, that the constraining import of the language derives solely from the words on the page.[14] It is as though the word "handicap" has a meaning attached to it, apart from what the speaker is trying to do by using the word. It does not matter whether one is playing golf, predicting the way the ponies are going to finish at Santa Anita, or trying to prevent discrimination on the job. It is as though all words were proper nouns. With good cause, Wittgenstein railed against this referential theory of meaning.

Without context and implicit purpose, there is no meaning.[15] At least one would like to be so radical in rejecting the tempting but primitive view that words carry their meanings around with them. Perhaps there are some exceptions, such as proper nouns, but surely the more plausible view of communication in language stresses the shared context between speaker and hearer. The context includes an understanding, based on life experience, about what the speaker's purposes might be. When we confront a sign that tells us "No vehicles in the park" we understand what the speaker is trying to tell us. Because we grasp the context and purpose, we can confidently follow the sign's instructions. Suppose, however, the sign at the entrance to the park read: "Keep off the cracks in the sidewalk." These words, taken individually, are rather precise, but there is no way to discern what the speaker is after. We don't know what the Park Department is trying to forbid and why. Does "keep off" mean, "don't step on" or does it mean "don't stand on" or "don't sit on?" But even if the sign were formulated, "Do not sit on . . . " we would be equally nonplused. What does sitting amount to? Is an inch of overlap enough to say that one is sitting on the crack? If the command seems arbitrary, if we do not understand the point of it, then there is no way to make it precise.

Precision is not a function of words, but of a shared understanding that invests the words with sense in the particular context. Suppose a sign at a turnstile reads, "Do not play on the turnstile." This seems clear enough, but let us suppose a couple of senior citizens are looking for a place to set up their chessboard. Do they violate the instruction if they lay the board on top of the turnstile? The world "play" is surely ambiguous and "play on," even more so. Yet in the context the command is clear. It is not the words that make it clear, but a shared understanding that it is dangerous for kids to jump and swing on turnstiles.

Prohibitions are designed for routine and normal cases. And in these cases, their point is usually clear. But it is not the statute that creates the normal case. Rather it is the prestatutory, shared sense of normalcy that enables us to say that statutory language clearly prohibits certain forms of conduct.

The principle of *nulla poena sine lege*—statutory warning must precede the commission of a crime—articulates the minimal demand of the rule of law for criminal prosecutions. The warning must be sufficiently specific to enable people to guide their conduct and avoid criminal liability. This is the basic principle of a liberal system of criminal law, liberal because it takes for granted dissention and pluralistic conceptions of right and wrong.

We could hardly make sense of this imperative unless it were restricted to the standard and normal cases of each prohibition. It is fairly clear what the prohibitions against homicide and theft are designed to prevent. Once we consider the abnormal cases covered by the defenses, such as self-defense and necessity, the factual possibilities become so numerous that the prohibition loses its apparent specificity. The defense of necessity, for example, permits a defense to theft whenever the lesser evil under the circumstances is to take an object belonging to another. Suppose that this defense were included in the prohibition so that it read: "do not steal unless it is the lesser evil to do so." If a potential thief had to analyze each factual situation to decide whether it was the greater good (lesser evil) to steal or not to steal, the prohibition would hardly have bite.

The core elements of each offense point to the normal case; the defenses, the claims of justification and excuse, come into play only in abnormal situations. This structuring of the rules of criminal law generates a field of application for the imperative *nulla poena sine lege*. The imperative of legislative warning attaches most clearly to the core elements of the prohibition, the normal cases of wrongdoing. This is why the grand prohibitions of the criminal law—"do not kill," "do not steal," "do not hit," and the like—are formulated without reference to the exceptional situations in which these forms of aggression might be justified or excused.

The point of this discussion is to demonstrate that the pragmatic-agnostic view of the rule of law is plausible, but that the view requires a serious reorientation. The emphasis in the literature on the controlling effect of language will not do. A clear and precise prohibition presupposes a shared understanding of the point of prohibiting particular conduct. It is not the statute that informs us what not to do, but our prestatutory understanding of normalcy and sensible prohibitions that enables us to follow legislative commands.

II. Equality

We may conclude that if the "believer's" conception of the rule of law is not compelling, at least the pragmatic agnostic's view, as modified in the argument above, merits our respect. Yet it is difficult to reduce the rule of law to the simple claim that the legislature can effectively control human conduct by laying down rules that govern normal cases. Something must be implicit in a value that has moved so many reformers' spirits in this century.

That additional value component does not lend itself to consensus. One would be hard pressed to maintain that the rule of law presupposes the protection of the American Bill of Rights or even, more modestly, of the due process clause. Yet, as I will argue, one significant value, the principle of equality, does inhere in the rule of law.

The principle of equality functions as a restraint on the kinds of rules that are acceptable, even if enacted by the legislature. The principle requires that if two categories of people are apparently alike, then they must receive the same treatment. Differential treatment is unacceptable unless a convincing distinction between the two categories is available. The phrases "apparently alike" and "convincing distinction" admittedly require some fleshing out. To clarify these phrases and the analysis of equality, I propose that we take a closer look at a 1988 proposal to reform a Soviet statute on capital punishment.

THE BALANCE OF FREEDOM

Under the former Soviet criminal codes, seventeen offenses were potentially punished by the firing squad. These included embezzling state property in large quantities, serious cases of bribery, violating the currency laws, and counterfeiting. In the fever for reform under *perestroika*, liberals proposed limiting capital punishment to six offenses: treason, espionage, terrorism, sabotage, intentional and aggravated homicide, and the rape of a minor. There was a good chance that the last category would be dropped, which means that capital punishment would be confined to what appeared to be egregious offenses against the state and the most serious versions of homicide.[16]

In their zeal to freeze the trigger fingers of the firing squad, the reformers made some jurisprudential moves that raised questions about the Soviet commitment to the rule of law. The proposed new code categorically exempted three categories of offenders: minors under the age of 18, women as a class, and men who at the time of sentencing have reached the age of 60 years. It is hard to quarrel with compassion for the crimes of teenagers between the ages of 16 and 18, who arguably belong in the less punitive juvenile courts in any event. But the categorical exemptions for women and men over 60 leave one wondering whether the Soviet reformers understood what the rule of law is about.

In the course of a research sojourn in Moscow I pressed my Soviet colleagues for an explanation of the categorical exemption for women. I take it for granted that women and men are "apparently alike" and therefore, if they are to be treated differently, some convincing explanation is necessary. Six arguments recurred in my colleagues' efforts to justify differential treatment for women. First, the claim was that the exemption helped women but it did not hurt men; second, that it was better to abolish evil in part than to do nothing at all; third, that women are more emotional than men; fourth, that women played a special role in Soviet society as mothers and housewives; fifth, that women were never executed for capital offenses anyway, and finally, sixth, that it was important to limit capital punishment as much as possible and exempting women was a politically feasible way of doing so. These arguments are worth reviewing in detail.

The first argument, that the exemption helped women without hurting men, assumes that as a result of the exemption for men, the same number, certainly no more men would face the firing squad. Therefore men as a class were not hurt and women benefitted. What could be wrong with that?

The only thing wrong with it is that it violates the principle of equality. The violation becomes obvious if we shift our focus away from gender distinctions to areas where reactions are more likely to be intuitive and automatic. Suppose the Soviet government had decided to cut back the use of capital punishment by exempting a racial or national minority or by singling out for preferential treatment some group defined by a random physical characteristic, such as eye or hair color. This would have been blatant discrimination and most lawyers would be so repelled by the arbitrariness of the classification that they would reject it out of hand.

But not everyone would. I encountered a surprising number of lawyers, passionately opposed to capital punishment, who reasoned, as did the Soviet experts in their second move, that it is better to do the right thing with respect to half the population than not to do the right thing at all. If capital punishment is an evil, as most intellectuals seem to think these days, then abolishing part of the evil justified the partiality of the reform. Eventually, the reformers maintained, the repeal would have extended to everyone.

This argument challenges us to be clear about the imperative to treat everyone equally under the law. How strong an imperative is this? Is it absolute or must it be balanced against other worthy goals, such as cutting back the use of capital punishment? And how do we go about deciding whether a differentiation in the statute constitutes impermissible discrimination? After all, if men and women are in fact different, lumping them together in one category is also unjust.

THE BALANCE OF FREEDOM

The problem with gender distinctions is that they are sometimes justified. While it is very rare that we justify differential treatment on the basis of race or random physical characteristics, it makes sense in some situations to single out women as a class. The Soviet Basic Principles of Criminal Legislation recognized other forms of special treatment for our traditionally more domestic and gentler sex. The new forms of confinement—isolation and limited freedom, introduced in the reformed law as a substitute for domestic exile—cannot be imposed either against pregnant women or against women with children under the age of eight. Recognizing the special role of women as mothers makes sense where women are in fact pregnant or acting as caretakers of young children. But it does not follow that all women, whether married or not, whether mothers or not, warrant special treatment in a system of punishment.

The proper mode of proceeding is to ask the point of the distinction between men and women in a particular context and then to inquire whether there is some gender-based characteristic that justifies the differential treatment. If the issue is assuring that young children are properly cared for, it makes sense to exempt women with young children from certain modes of punishment. Perhaps it is all right as well to recognize that for purposes of insuring minimally acceptable prison conditions, women as a class are less hardy than men and are likely to suffer more from the same amount of physical deprivation. Of course, these kinds of generalizations cut a wide swath. It is difficult to say whether in this context gender-based categories are impermissibly overinclusive.

The minimal condition for justifying differential treatment is that the proponent point to some characteristic of the privileged group as the basis for the differential treatment. Then the argument must turn first on whether the privileged group in fact possesses the relevant characteristic and second whether the alleged characteristic justifies the differential treatment. Two examples illustrate the required process of argument. Some Russian scholars I spoke with claimed, as the third argument of the six, that the exemption for women found its warrant in the inclination of women to be more emotional. Even if we could render this claim more precise and we accepted it, it is hard to see why the emotions of women should exempt them from the death penalty. Perhaps the argument is that women, like children, are not fully responsible for their crimes. If that is the case, then women, like children, should be subject to trial in courts of special jurisdiction. Perhaps the story is that in waiting out their days on death row, women suffer more than men do; therefore as applied to women, capital punishment is even crueler than when applied to men. The argument fails to convince me, for even if some women might have these sensibilities, it is not clear that female murderers do; if they did, they might have been less inclined to kill.

Another problematic distinction is often invoked to justify the discrimination implicit in statutory rape statutes. A man who seduces a young woman commits a serious crime, but an older woman who seduces a young boy does not. Now we all know why this discrimination is built into the law, but no one today is willing to admit the residue of Victorian morality in our legal thinking. The more fashionable argument is that the male seducer exposes the young female to a risk of pregnancy, but the female seducer does not.[17] There is no doubt that this is true. The problem is whether the reed is strong enough to carry the full weight of a categorical distinction between male and female seducers.

Both of these difficult cases strike me as different from the problem of preferred treatment for women under the selective service laws of most countries. Typically, men are drafted, women are not.[18] This differentiation cannot be justified on the ground that women are weaker and not generally suitable for combat missions (although that too is contestable); modern military operations require numerous people in noncombat (i.e., office) positions wherein women can perform obviously as well as if not better than men. If there is a justification for exempting women from the draft, it would have to run something like this: Women serve their country as mothers and housewives. Men should serve their country by protecting it against foreign enemies. Hard as it may be to believe, this is about all there is to say about a practice that is taken for granted in the Western democracies.

The same style of argument comes into play in the fourth move made on behalf of the exemption of women from capital punishment. Women serve their country as mothers and housewives. It is only fitting that men serve in a different capacity, namely as the fodder fed to a system designed to deter crime and maintain public order. For good or ill, Oliver Wendell Holmes, Jr., drew the analogy between a convicted criminal headed for the gallows and a soldier going off to war. Both serve a higher goal called the public good. If this analogy were really convincing, then we might have a case for having only men bear the brunt of the system of deterrence by capital execution.

When none of these other arguments have the desired impact, advocates for the exemption are likely to fall back on the sociological insight: "As a matter of practice, women are never executed anyway. The proposed legislation merely ratifies the status quo." This is another way of claiming, "We are not really doing anything; so how can we be doing anything wrong?" This is the most intriguing argument of all, and one that one often hears in debates about the reform of the criminal law. Suppose that in setting bail judges implicitly consider the risk that the suspect will commit an offense before trial. Does it follow that the risk of recidivism becomes a ground for openly and explicitly denying access to bail? Suppose that in analyzing the constitutionality of police searches, the courts implicitly considered the gravity of the offense charged against the defendant; in murder cases they reach results that they would probably not favor in gun possession cases. Does it follow that in all cases, the gravity of the crime charged should become a factor relevant to the constitutionality of the search? And if as a matter of practice, women are never executed, does that fact alone make it permissible to make the exemption official by writing it into the statute?

There are two quick ways to counter this move that whatever is done implicitly may also be done explicitly. First, we need only shift the focus again to a suspect categorization. Let us suppose that a particular minority in the former USSR, say the Uzbeks, had never been subject to the firing squad. Could one write in an exception for them? Surely, the contingent fact that no Uzbek had ever been sentenced to death could hardly support a judgment that it was right, in principle, to treat Uzbeks differently. What is at stake is the difference between a contingent practice and a reasoned basis for differential treatment.

Second, if the practice is truly invariable, if there is no risk that a woman would be condemned to death, then there is no need to legislate on the matter. The response to this perfectly sensible point, and one that the Soviet reformers would have likely made, is that the law serves an educational as well as a regulative function. It was important to accustom people to the idea that capital punishment was on the way out, both as to the range of offenses punished and as to the domain of offenders subject to execution.

This emphasis on the educational value of the reform appears in the sixth and final argument, namely that exempting women from the death penalty was a desirable step toward its abolition that the public was willing to accept. If the public could accept sparing women, they would arguably come closer to exempting men as well. In the end, this was probably the decisive argument in favor of the proposal. Its significance lay in the implicit concession that indeed there is no convincing basis for the distinction between men and women. Men suffer discrimination for the sake of social progress—in this case, the total abolition of capital punishment.

III. Conclusion

The rule of law imposes a constraint on the direct pursuit of political goals, such as the abolition of capital punishment.

Enacting rules that exempt women may further this goal, but rules that discriminate between men and women, without adequate explanation, seem to collapse legislation into opportunistic politics and thus call into question whether the rule of law is being observed.

I cannot say for sure that the principle of equality is immanent in the rule of law. It might simply be a desirable principle, like freedom of speech, that any civilized legal system would adopt. In the end, it is hard to know what the evidence would be that would settle one interpretation or the other. Dworkin's analysis of law as integrity implicitly supports the view that equality and consistency are essential components of the idea of law.[19] He reasons that most people committed to law would, in the case of capital punishment, for example, reject a partial reform, a checkerboard solution, as lacking integrity and consistency.

But I wonder whether this is true. I have talked to numerous American academic lawyers who say they agree with the Soviet reformers: in the face of great evil, a partial reform is better than no reform at all. Many people say that capital punishment differs from other issues, but does it? I suspect with the passions running high on the issue of abortion, many people would accept an inconsistent partial concession to their side—say prohibiting, or permitting, abortion in alternate weeks—rather than suffer a total loss. What is true about the death penalty and abortion would also prevail in other sensitive political areas. I agree with Dworkin that a checkerboard solution violates the basic principle of consistency implicit in the rule of law. Would that lawyers and other citizens agreed.

A critical aspect of the rule of law is the ongoing process of dialogue, or reason-giving, of the disciplined attempt by judges to justify their decisions under the law. The effort to justify distinctions, as in my discussions about the Soviet capital punishment proposal, is a critical part of that process.

Dialogue requires respect for the opposition, and that, unfortunately, is what is missing in the argument that a partial reform is better than no reform at all. The assumption seems to be that capital punishment is so evil that any measure to curtail it would be justified. But that attribution of evil ignores that the majority of the public in most democratic societies today still favors capital punishment. The movement toward abolition is maintained and fostered by legal elites around the world.

When one begins to treat the opposition as a pack of evildoers, then the rule of law gives way to bargaining with a perceived devil. In the end, the maintenance of the rule of law is a matter of tolerance and reciprocal respect. If there is any message to be conveyed today to those who wish to further the rule of law, I would put it simply: treat the opposition as rational, as open to persuasion, and seek to bring about change, not by haphazard political gains, but by convincing the opposition that you are right.

NOTES

1. 29 U.S.C. at 794, § 504.
2. 480 U.S. 273 (1987).
3. See Dworkin, *The Model of Rules*, 35 U.Chi.L.Rev 14 (1967).
4. 480 U.S. at 284.
5. This is the term used in the statute to define handicap. See 29 U.S.C. 706 (7)(B).
6. The decision does not resolve the question whether an HIV positive, who was not impaired in daily functioning, should be similarly classified. Id. at 282 n.7.
7. Id. at 489 (Rehnquist, C.J. dissenting)
8. As the dissent saw the problem, the statute should be construed strictly on the ground that, as held in Pennhurst State School and Hospital v. Halderman, 451 U.S. 1 (1981), the conditions for federal funding imposed by the Rehabilitation Act function like a contract between private parties. The recipients should be held to have agreed not to discriminate against tuberculosis carriers only if that

condition is clearly and unequivocally imposed by the statute. 480 U.S. at 489-90.

9. For a fuller version of this interpretation, see Fletcher, *Two Modes of Legal Thought*, 90 Yale L.J. 970 (1981).

10. See, e.g., Unger, *The Critical Studies Movement*, 96 Harv. L. Rev. 561, 563-76 (1983); Singer, *The Player and the Cards: Nihilism and Legal Theory*, 94 Yale L.J. 1 (1984).

11. See Unger, supra note 10; M. Kelman, *A Guide to Critical Legal Studies* (1988).

12. Weinrib, *Legal Formalism: On the Immanent Rationality of Law*, 97 Yale L.J. 949 (1988).

13. Schauer, *Formalism*, 97 Yale L.J. 509 (1988).

14. Schauer, supra note 13, at 528 ("[M]eaning can be 'acontextual' in the sense that it draws on no other context besides those understandings shared by among virtually all speakers of English.")

15. For some clever reflections on the relationship between meaning and context, see S. Fish, *Is There a Text in this Class?* (1980).

16. This picture is slightly misleading, however, for treason is likely to retain a broad definition, which includes various innocuous acts such as illegally leaving the country with the intent to weaken Soviet power.

17. See Michael M. v. Sonoma County, 453 U.S. 460 (1981).

18. For a test case on the issue of draft registration, see Roster v. Goldberg, 453 U.S. 57 (1981).

19. R. Dworkin, *Law's Empire.* (1986).

FOUR

THE RULE OF LAW
IN A THEORETICAL
AND COMPARATIVE
PERSPECTIVE

Andrzej Rapaczynski

The principle of the rule of law has some rather simple and intuitive meanings which very few today are prepared to question. In committing ourselves to the idea of a *Rechtsstaat* or in saying that we want "a government of laws and not of men," we often mean that we do not want our governments to exercise arbitrary power over us. This intuition, which is probably the most central for the understanding of the principle of the rule of law, expresses our distrust of absolute power: the rulers should tell us in advance what they demand from us, they should have sufficient general reasons why they want us to do or not to do something, and they should be held to their word. In this sense, the rule of law is the cardinal principle of *political freedom.*

The rule of law is seen as not only a principle of freedom, but also of equality, since another of its simple meanings is that the generality of the law requires that people in similar circumstances should be treated similarly, so that no one is singled out for a specially favorable or unfavorable treatment, unless for some reason of general validity.

There is, I am sure, a number of other intuitive connotations of the principle, such as, for example, the dignitary value of not being subjected to the rule of other people, but rather of being treated as an adult obeying rational principles of action embodied in the laws of the community. But I shall not enumerate them, since the ones already mentioned are enough to make us see (in the unlikely case we had not done so before) that the rule of law is commonly seen as a foundation of any civilized political community.

It is quite possible, however, to take a much more skeptical view of the rule of law, and I wonder why it is so rarely done. It is a characteristic of our attachment to the idea of the rule of law that we are prepared to believe that the very form of legality has some significant consequences for the nature of political action. Someone could say, however, that the principle of the rule of law has no effect whatever on whether a government allows its citizens any freedom or treats them as equals in any morally significant sense. Indeed, unless we are not prepared to recognize the validity or "true" legality of those positive laws that do not conform to some substantive principles of *Recht* or "natural justice," the rule of law may be equally well the rule of bad or evil laws as that of good and decent ones. To be sure, respect for the rule of law does limit the rulers somewhat, in that they may be forced to attend to certain procedures, but it also allows them to reap the benefits of a certain amount of stability that may be of use to tyrants and democrats alike. Why are we then predisposed to believe that the very form of legality has some normatively significant political efficacy?

Another reason why someone may doubt the importance of the idea of the rule of law is connected not with the fact that the laws themselves may be evil as well as good, but rather with the fact that they are, as Hobbes said, just words and thus not enough to stop any tyrant from doing the mischief he intends. The reason for this is not just what Hobbes thought, namely, that words can be broken; the more serious problem is that they can, indeed must, be interested. And since interpretation does not have any *a priori* boundaries, i.e., since no text has meaning all by itself, independently from the context in which it is read, he who controls the process of interpretation controls the substantive outcome as well. In what sense, then, could we expect the very form of the law to protect us against governmental oppression?

I believe that these concerns of the skeptics with respect to the idea of the rule of law must be taken seriously. I do not intend to "debunk" the idea, in the sense of showing that it is completely delusory, but neither do I think we can retain the lofty notion of the law, in which some quite realistic concerns are left unaddressed. Moreover, while the rule of law certainly has very considerable merits, unless its very concept is properly analyzed, we are apt to underestimate a number of other mechanisms equally (and in some situations better) able to achieve similar goals.

There are, we ought to realize at the outset, two quite distinct threads involved in the ideal of the rule of law. The first is the philosophical one, associated with such figures as Rousseau and Kant. The second, much less glamorous, views the rule of law as related to the idea of a bureaucratic state, characteristic of the more modern societies. It is to this second, less glamorous incarnation of the rule of law that I want to give its due.

The philosophical conception of the rule of law is based not on any empirical observation concerning the nature of the political process, but rather on a theory of moral action which *a priori* prescribes a norm for political arrangements. Both Rousseau and Kant identified the form of legality with the very rationality of human action: an action according to a law is not an unreflective, *ad hoc* response to some particular stimulation (such as is characteristic of the behavior of animals), not a selfish, unreflective reaction to the world outside, but a considered human response, mediated by reference to a general principle, valid for all similar situations. According to these philosophers, the difference between an unfree, heteronomous behavior and a morally significant, free, or autonomous action is that the former is merely a more or less mechanical effect of environmental factors, while the latter is a consequence of the uniquely human capacity to reason. And the idea of a law-abiding action is supposed to express precisely this rationality bound character of human freedom.

Viewed in this light, the rule of law is not just an instrument of human freedom, say, a method of preventing the rulers from preferring their particularistic interests to the interests of the community as a whole. It is rather an end worth pursuing for its own sake, one that a tyrant forgoes not only at the peril of his subjects' liberty, but as Plato had argued, his own as well. For the law of the community, according to a Rousseau or a Kant, is but an objectified form of the inner commands of reason and morality, the obedience to which raises us above the level of animals. Moreover, in the Rousseauean and Kantian frameworks, the so called "evil laws" are in some sense not laws at all; the very purpose of the law is to enable man to live in freedom and equality, so that laws that subvert this ideal are only spuriously laws; in fact, they represent surreptitious ways of pursuing the very particularistic interests which it was the purpose of the law to eliminate in favor of the interests of the rational human community.

As opposed to this philosophical view of the rule of law, the other perspective, which I want to develop here, begins from the admission that law is inherently coercive: it is in fact only one of the many devices of political power designed to force an individual to deviate from what he or she may be otherwise inclined to do. This does not mean, of course, that the law is always evil or that it is always imposed on the individuals against their own will: it might very well be that individuals might view the price of obeying the law worth paying in exchange for the advantage of constraining the behavior of others, and they might thus accept it as ultimately in their best interest. But this means only that coercion may sometimes be justified, not that it is the very essence of freedom.

Law is, however, a special tool in the arsenal of governmental coercion, distinct from personal authority or naked physical force, and in order to understand how the rule of law may affect social reality, we must keep in mind the specific function of legal norms. Now, I do not have a theory that would cover all possible aspects of the nature of law, but whatever else it may be, in every imperfect society the law is also a way of economizing on honesty, skill, and expertise. In a perfect society, i.e., a group of perfectly rational and moral agents with free access to all relevant information, there might be no need for the law as a distinct discipline: citizens (and judges in particular, if there were to be such) would simply do what is right, without any need to refer to a set of preexisting general rules of conduct. To be sure, there would still be a need for political theory, economics, perhaps even philosophy: these would be the very things the agents would have to know in order to do what is right; but there would be no need of codifying any of this knowledge in the form of the law. The only exception would be when all would agree that, for the purpose of coordination, there should be some general rule of conduct (such as that one should drive on the left side of the street, for example), although it did not matter what the rule would be. In such a situation, if no "invisible hand" were to lead to the adoption of one rule or another a "political" decision would have to be made that all would later obey.

One might think that the law would become necessary when people could no longer be viewed as perfectly moral or honest. But that is not necessarily the case. To be sure, the moral fall of man would likely yield the need for some form of authority, akin to the state, to keep the weak and evil in check. But so long as people were still perfectly rational (and in possession of cost less information), everyone would immediately know what is right and what is wrong, so that the only command of the authorities would be "Do what is right." Now, I do not think that a skeletal command system like that would deserve the name of the law, except in the most Pickwickian, ultra-positivist sense, since there would still be no independent substance to the orders sent down from on high, nor any particular form in which such orders would have to be issued or enforced.

What makes a legal system truly necessary is the relaxation of the assumption of perfect rationality (or perfect information). Once it can no longer be assumed that the people interested in a certain social outcome can agree on the proper choice and application of a body of knowledge necessary for its achievement, and once a person entrusted with a task no longer knows how to go about accomplishing it, the state's desire to control the behavior of particular social actors or to empower a decision maker to resolve the conflicts among them implies that the authorities must come up with a detailed set of instructions controlling both the substance and the procedure of a variety of social interactions.

These instructions could be of several kinds. The state could, for example, try to educate each actor, be it a private party or a government official, about its view of the significance of his actions and their various socially desirable or undesirable consequences. Once in possession of that knowledge, the actor could then be taught how to weigh the relative merits of all these outcomes *vis à vis* all the other socially relevant factors and instructed to maximize whatever values the authorities wanted to maximize. But that would be a very cumbersome way of going about doing the government's business. First, in the world of imperfectly rational agents, the people to whom the state's instructions are directed may be unable not only to figure out for themselves the desirable courses of action, but also to understand the complex instructions they are given. (This would be especially true in a society in which people are not only imperfectly, but also differentially rational, i.e., when different individuals have vastly different capacities in different fields of knowledge or activity.) But, second, and more important, even if it were possible to teach everyone why and how the state may want to regulate the social consequences of his actions, to do so would be extremely wasteful, and certain goals could be achieved much more cost-effectively by simply ordering particular actors to conform to relatively simple rules, without any need to rely on the actors' understanding of their purposes or the social consequences of their actions.

The law, while it may also be something more than this, is in any case such a system of instructions and procedures regulating the behavior of social actors, a system which translates the socially available knowledge about the way society works and should be governed into a language that can be more readily accessible to its addressees and permits us to accumulate and store further information relating to particular instances of social behavior.

Another way of expressing the same idea is the following: Societies need to routinize their ways of dealing with problems that recur with a certain frequency, so that solutions once adopted can then be reapplied without going through the costly process of devising them again. The law is, above all, a repository of such routines, together with a routinized method of applying them to new cases and arriving at new variations of the old solutions. In this sense, law is inherently tied to the phenomenon of bureaucracy. Even in the simplest system, in which people come to a certain person, such as a tribal chief or a village elder, in order to have him resolve their controversies, or in which the ruler decides on the fate of those who disobey him (or some religious or moral command that the ruler intends to uphold), we can start speaking of a "legal system" only when the decider, instead of approaching each problem anew, adopts some uniform routinized methods (involving substantive and procedural rules) of resolving the cases before him. In a more complex society, such rules can themselves become quite complicated, so as to require a whole class of professionals (lawyers, judges, administrators, and other kinds of bureaucrats) to interpret them, and it may sometimes happen that the whole system becomes so cumbersome as to appear to be more difficult to administer than devising new solutions *ab ovo*. Such times are those of revolution or legal reform. But normally, the *ratio essendi* of a legal system is that, complicated as it may be, the bureaucratic system makes the job of social control more efficient.

If we adopt this rather deflationary account of what the law is, it becomes somewhat less self-evident why the rule of law is seen as something worthy of so much veneration. If our preference for it survives, it must be because the bureaucratic form of government has some inherent advantages over its competitors.

Despite the decisively moral tone in which the rule of law is usually defended, the advantages of bureaucratic administration are primarily pragmatic and efficiency related. The development of bureaucracy, and consequently the expansion of the legal domain, is above all a function of increasing social complexity, rather than a morally driven phenomenon. Without the increasing social complexity, the demand for good government could just as well take the form of a demand for rulers personally committed to moral or religious righteousness, rather than limited by legal norms. The same demand could not, however, be expected to yield a desirable political order in a more complex system; here a recourse to legal restraints seems to be a necessity. To be sure, even under modern conditions, the law is only a necessary but not sufficient condition of good government; there remains always the possibility of a government of evil laws. But in most systems in which the question of the rule of law is a live one, the laws are presumed not to be in principle evil, since they are thought to express the will of the legitimate, sovereign authority (nowadays often believed to be the "people," though in practice the laws are enacted by various bodies subject to a more or less effective system of electoral control), and that authority's legitimacy means that its will to do what is good is not seriously in doubt. The bureaucracy executing the laws is, on the other hand, usually viewed as a body alien to the people and systematically prone to substitute its own interest, or the private interests of its members, for the interest of the ruled. The law is thus viewed as the most important barrier against governmental exploitation, the mechanism by which the people (or, in the old times, the good king) keeps its (his) evil servants in check.

To what extent does this picture of law-restrained bureaucracy reflect the political reality of modern states? Is it true that, on the one hand, the law genuinely stands for the element of virtue or public interest in the community and, on the other hand, the bureaucracy acting without a legal norm represents the forces of oppression and exploitation? The truth seems to me much more complicated.

Let us begin with the association of law and public interest. There are surely many cases in which such an association is warranted. The most obvious cases are those in which the law prohibits socially destructive behavior (such as murder, assault, or robbery) or in which it is obviously directed against free riding (the punishing of tax or draft evasion, for example). But the interesting cases, in which the relation between the law and the public interest is potentially much more problematic, are not those in which the law enforces clearly preexisting social norms or coordinates individual behavior to achieve unquestioned general benefits. They are rather cases in which public policy is made, i.e., those in which the goals to be pursued are not clearly defined and a decision must be made as to what is or is not in the public interest and whether or not it should be pursued by means of a collective, political action, involving (in contradistinction to a market solution) an element of governmental compulsion. Now, in these types of cases, the idea that the sovereign (in the old days the king, and nowadays the people) "can do no wrong," and that the source of all evil lies with bad advisers (bureaucrats), is seriously open to question. We need not assume that virtue is altogether absent from political life in order to maintain that run-of-the-mill political events are dominated by the struggle among various groups intent on accomplishing through the political what they are incapable of achieving on their own. Manufacturers hanker after freedom from competition and coercively enforced price agreements, farmers want price supports, professionals desire barriers to entry, consumers fight for lower prices, groups with moralistic programs covet compulsory compliance with their value preferences, and no doubt about it, bureaucrats yearn for higher budgets and greater regulatory powers. It may be an important factor in legitimating a political system to believe that the ultimate sovereign would never freely choose a particularistic private interest over the good of the public. But quite apart from any hypothesis of an evil tyrant, it was always more or less a fiction that "the king can do no wrong," and the goodness of the people is a principle of not much greater realism. The laws get passed not because "the people" decide something, but because of struggles and compromises, many of which are very much the effect of a capture of the state apparatus for the benefit of a particular faction. The laws' formal status of being properly enacted may be enough to make most people obey them, but it is quite easy to imagine that the public interest would be better served by their absence. It is in fact not very hard to imagine that a well-trained bureaucrat endowed with appropriate discretion may do a better job at distributing certain scarce goods than a legislature composed of members sorely in need of campaign funds for their reelection.

Furthermore, the very idea that law is a restraint on the otherwise inherent arbitrariness of bureaucratic administration misstates the relation between legal norms and bureaucratic behavior. I said already that law is a system of routinized ways of dealing with problems that recur with certain frequency, together with a routinized method of applying them to new cases and arriving at new variations of the old solutions.

But this system cannot be limited to the propositions and doctrines contained in law books and statute collections. In fact, it is not impossible to imagine a legal system that has only a minimum of written law and relies predominantly on the orally delivered precedents stored in the memory of legal professionals. What this shows is that the personnel administering the law is very much a component of the legal system, perhaps its most important component indeed. To rely on a legal system for the achievement of any social objective is, insofar as the law has to be executed, to rely on the bureaucracy which is charged with its enforcement.

This is not just a trivial point that someone must apply the law and that the people who do it are a part of state bureaucracy. Rather, the point I am trying to make is that law, as a mere text, is largely indeterminate, and that it is given life only in the process of its interpretation. The reason why all complex societies need a whole profession entrusted with the running of the legal system is that laymen are incapable of even understanding the meaning of legal norms, to say nothing of their proper application. The life of the law, therefore, is not the life of abstract norms and logical deductions, but a matter of professional skill in administering a complex institution. To be sure, one of the characteristic features of the law as a system of routinized solutions to recurring problems is that it allows a certain degree of hierarchical subordination, i.e., it gives those on the top of the bureaucratic hierarchy (the legislature, for example) a certain degree of control over the outcome of the whole arrangement. But that the law is capable of accomplishing anything meaningful at all is very much a byproduct of bureaucratic government and an internal characteristic of its mode of functioning. To view the law, therefore, as an external constraint on bureaucracy is to misunderstand the very nature of both.

Nor even insofar as the law is viewed as an internal mechanism of bureaucratic self-control, is it the only possible mechanism of this kind, or even the best one under all circumstances. Many people's ideas of bureaucracy have been shaped by the Weberian account of it, which views bureaucracy as a "purely" hierarchical arrangement, a transmission belt unidirectionally processing information from the bottom to the top and decisions from the top to the bottom. The law, in this model, is seen as a tool by which a complex task is divided into a number of separate components and sent down in the form of orders to the bureaucratic levels at which they are executed.

But the Weberian model is far from being the only one; in fact, it is not clear that any good bureaucracy actually functions in this way. A system of administration in which all decisions must be taken at the top is a system condemned to a degree of rigidity and central planning that makes the efficient accomplishment of any moderately complex task well-nigh impossible. It is true that bureaucratic decision making is only necessary when ordinary market solutions do not work and it is thus not possible to assume that individual actions will be spontaneously coordinated to yield the optimal result. In this sense, bureaucracy always presupposes some artificial coordination mechanism, normally established by means of the law. But within this framework, the coordination of the actions of individual bureaucrats does not have to proceed exclusively by a system of centrally designed routines, sent from the top and frozen until revoked. Another method is to create such conditions for the operation of the lower levels of the bureaucracy that the personal interests of the actors (their desire to advance within the administrative hierarchy, their prestige, material rewards, and the "perks" of their office) are synchronized with the performance advancing the goals for which the bureau was created. If this is accomplished, a lower level bureaucrat, instead of being controlled as narrowly as possible by the prescribed routines of his office, can be given a significant amount of discretion in order to use his special familiarity and expertise with the matters entrusted to him for their resolution. In such conditions, when lower level bureaucratic posts involve a significant amount of responsibility, capable individuals may be more easily drawn into public service, and they can be relied upon to exercise in their work those peculiar managerial skills that would otherwise be lost, since they resist codification in a set of explicit general rules (such as "must be used by the law"). The bureaucrats can then also adapt their solutions to the changing nuances of a particular case, as well as generally use their creativity in order to improve the functioning of their office.

That the method of creating an appropriate set of incentives may be a more efficient way of using the talents of an employee than putting him in a straightjacket of rigid rules and superior commands is a truism in most private corporations which, like state bureaucracies, replace ordinary market mechanisms with artificially created structures of hierarchical organization. A manager of a General Motors' subsidiary (as well as many much lower level officers), instead of being told in painstaking detail how to do his job, is usually given certain basic parameters within which he must operate and be informed that his compensation and advancement will depend on the results with which he uses the means at his disposal. To be sure, most state bureaucracies differ in significant respects from for-profit corporations, not least because their products (such as justice, national defense, or the quality of life) are often rather difficult to define in the abstract, and consequently it is very difficult to devise quantitative, or even qualitative, criteria of good bureaucratic performances. This in turn means that a synchronization of the bureaucrat's private interests with the interests of his bureau may present serious difficulties: unlike the General Motors' manager, whose performance can often be measured on the account books of the corporation by the value of the products contributed by the unit under his command, a bureaucrat cannot easily be told that his rewards will depend on the value of the services he provides, since the real value of these services is often very difficult to determine. Despite this fact, the cost of eliminating the bureaucrat's spontaneity from the motoric forces of the bureaucratic machine is simply too high, even if the methods of harnessing it into the service of the public are on the whole less efficacious than in the private sector. Some degree of the inefficiency of public bureaucracy may perhaps be lessened by the bureaucrat's long-term integration in a large body of other public servants united by the ties of a strong professional culture. The *esprit de corps* of the large group and its code of professional behavior may then direct the bureaucrat's efforts away from his purely particularistic interests and focus them on earning the long-term rewards of his profession. Devising a number of competing bureaucratic structures which may watch over each other's performance is sometimes also an additional method of controlling bureaucratic arbitrariness. But ultimately, some degree of governmental inefficiency must perhaps be simply tolerated and calculated into the price of the services it provides.

The consequences of all this for our subject are the following. The bureaucrat's discretion, even considering the likelihood of a certain degree of its abuse, is one of the most valuable elements of any well functioning administration. Consequently, it is not always true that replacing governmental discretion with legal constraints is a good thing. To be sure, the framework within which a bureaucrat operates must be established by law. But how much of his day-to-day operations similarly should be determined and how much should be a matter of his judgment, based on special familiarity and expertise, depends on a number of factors, and different bureaucratic systems may differ quite a lot in their preferences for one or the other mode of operation. Some, which value predictability or legislative supremacy, opt for more legal restraints. Others, which stress competence and expertise, opt for more bureaucratic discretion. And all vary their mix of constraint and discretion depending on the task to be accomplished.

A few examples may bring out more clearly the tradeoffs involved in the relation between discretion and constraint.

Nowhere perhaps is the rule of law thought to be more important than in the area of criminal law: no one can be convicted of a crime, it is said, without there having been a prior law making his conduct punishable. One reason why this is so is that the accused must have had some notice of the criminality of his conduct, some warning without which he cannot be held criminally responsible. Undoubtedly, in the case of the conduct that has been lawful and more or less commonly engaged in for a while the principle of legality makes eminent sense: it would violate our elementary sense of justice if a person who invested his money abroad, for example, were to be put in jail because his government, faced with a deteriorating balance of trade, suddenly and without warning changed its mind about allowing taking its currency abroad. But this consideration does not seem so weighty in the case of actions which are commonly considered criminal, although many people may not know exactly what the positive law of the country in which they find themselves does about them. It is hard to argue, for example, that a person (say, a visiting Frenchman, not versed in the English legal system) convicted of murder under the common law of England could really complain because at that time, as throughout most of the English history, no statutory enactments were necessary for a conviction. While this system may have produced some cases of injustice and we have now abandoned it, in many other situations it was not markedly inferior to most codified regimes.

But warning is not the only purpose of the principle of legality: prevention of governmental abuse is clearly another one. A citizen cannot be secure in his person and possessions, it is believed, unless he knows that his rulers cannot arbitrarily dispose of them in their own interests. Still, governmental abuse of the criminal process can be guarded against by means other than the presence of substantive criminal law. Here the example of the criminal common law of England is even more instructive. Even though the law of crimes was not codified in England, a very high degree of protection, indeed higher than in most other countries, was afforded to the defendant by the procedural aspects of trial and conviction, especially by the fact that the courts which tried him were independent of the legislature and the executive and had more interest in preserving their professional integrity than in serving the goals of the prosecution.

The case of the criminal common law of England is somewhat extreme: while it does show that an alternative to the principle of legality does not necessarily lead to any considerable degree of governmental oppression, our abandonment of it is, after all, some recognition of the superior desirability of a codified system. Still, the meaning of the principle of legality is in practice very different in the American system and in that of, say, Germany. In particular, a number of practices common in our system, such as prosecutorial discretion and plea bargaining, for example, are not only alien, but also quite distasteful to a German legal mind which is likely to see them as departures from the principle of the rule of law. Every system of criminal law must, of course, consider the ability of the judicial system to process the number of cases likely to be brought before it. Similarly, given that the high cost of processing criminal cases will make it impossible to prosecute all the cases one would want to prosecute in a cost less system, each actual system must set some priorities in deciding which cases to pursue and which to forgo. Now, plea bargaining and prosecutorial discretion are nothing other than ways of dealing with these problems by endowing public officials with a large amount of discretion: the prosecutor may simply optimize his efforts by deciding not to bring certain types of cases or by agreeing, in some other cases, to bring a lesser charge in exchange for a guilty plea on the part of the defendant. To be sure, there are various costs associated with this way of solving the problem: a certain number of innocent people may decide to plead guilty through fear of a higher penalty following a conviction, and the penalties for most crimes must be set higher than they would otherwise be in order both to give the defendant an incentive to settle and to preserve an adequate amount of deterrence in a system in which most defendants plead guilty and are convicted of a lesser offence. But not allowing these two discretionary methods of dealing with the overcrowding of the criminal process and replacing them with solutions in which each step of the prosecuting authorities is dictated by a fixed legal norm would have its costs too. Above all, abolition of plea bargaining and prosecutorial discretion would make it well-nigh impossible to preserve some of the most important procedural protection of our judicial system, such as the full-fledged adversarial jury trial and a realistic option for the defendant to refuse to collaborate in the preparation and presentation of the case against him, since these protections make trials extremely expensive and the system could not possibly process the number of cases required to effectuate the main purposes of the criminal law. As it is, while most defendants choose not to avail themselves of the protection of a full-fledged criminal trial, its rigors, its evidentiary rules, and the difficulty of conviction certainly increase the defendant's bargaining power and establish an element of control over the conduct of the prosecution. In societies with a relatively low crime rate, the abolition of plea bargaining and prosecutorial discretion might entail a compromise in terms of the quality of fair trials that might not be very significant, and the greater judicial efficiency of the civil law justice, for example, may very well be worth it in any case. But in societies with much larger crime rates, or in those in which the crime rate varies significantly over time and according to geographical location (as is the case in America), plea bargaining and prosecutorial discretion provide a very flexible tool of adjusting the "supply" of criminal justice to the changing "demand"; a tool without which trials would have to resemble much more an assembly line than a process with which lawyers are now familiar. Whether such a mass production of justice would be morally and politically more acceptable than the present system is a matter on which I prefer not to opine.

Consider another example in the area of criminal law that brings the tradeoff between flexibility and the rule of law into the starkest relief: the Nuremberg trials. Although some have tried to show otherwise, two of the counts of the indictment against the Nazi leaders had no precedent in international law: that of starting a war and that of genocide. Given this fact, the Allies faced three basic choices: they could let the behavior of the top Nazi leaders go unpunished, they could execute them simply as a matter of the right of the victors, or they could follow the path of the Nuremberg trials. Absolute adherence to the principle of legality would have to dictate the first course of action, since the absence of a clear preexisting legal norm would make a genuine trial impossible and the right of the victor, under international law, does not entail executing enemy leaders. The danger of an outright execution was to enshrine the principle of revenge. The danger of a trial was in a sense even greater: that of compromising the meaning of international criminal law and opening it for abuse by each victorious party in the future. But the arguments in favor of the trial were very strong as well: to let the Nazis go unpunished was a manifest injustice, for their actions were in significant ways not like that of any prior leaders of a country at war. The very war they started was unlike the previous ones; not only was it one of the purest and most unprovoked wars of aggression in history, but also its foreseeable destructiveness, particularly with respect to civilians, was so entirely unprecedented as to make it self-evidently criminal. Furthermore, the mass persecution and murder of entire peoples on the basis of their race, even when engaged in under the cover of legal norms that would be formally valid under national and international law, was so obviously violative of the basic principles of justice that no warning in the form of a legal norm had been really necessary. To be sure, the judges were the victors and the hands of some of them were far from clean, thus detracting somewhat from the appearances of righteousness in their actions. But over all, it is at least arguable that the Nuremberg trials, even if they violated the normal understanding of the principle of legality, were a stark example of the victory of justice over the rigid adherence to the rule of law.

Consider a further example, this time drawn from the extremely sensitive area of state security. Imagine a situation in which leaders of a dangerous terrorist group, who find themselves in jail, are suspected by the authorities of using their privileged communications with their attorneys in order to continue directing the operations of their comrades still at large, including planning new terrorist attacks and escape attempts. The legal system of the country in which this occurs is committed to a very strong principle of the rule of law, and consequently, the police officials have very little discretion in selecting what they consider the most effective methods of dealing with the threat involved.

A situation very much like this arose in West Germany some years ago in connection with the so-called Baader-Meinhof group. Ultimately, the then justice minister decided to install listening devices in the rooms in which the suspects communicated with their lawyers, but he did it without any legal justification. When the matter became public, he tendered his resignation, describing his actions as a form of civil disobedience in defense of the moral value of combating terrorism. I understand that his resignation was ultimately not accepted, but his action was universally viewed as incompatible with the principle of the rule of law in the German state.

When a German friend of mine was telling me about this case and I expressed my astonishment at a system in which something like this was necessary, he exclaimed somewhat agitated: "You Americans do not know what a *Rechtsstaat* is; you know about fairness, but not about the rule of law!" Thinking back about this, I see that he had a point: should a situation like this arise in the United States, I can think of several outcomes, but I can more or less exclude the one just recounted. Like in Germany, the threat of governmental abuse might not be dealt with through a special statutory entitlement, since intrusion into the privacy of attorney client privilege, particularly in a criminal defense context, is a very serious matter and it would be very difficult, if not outright impossible, to give a clear statutory authorization to eavesdrop which could not be easily abused. But precisely because of this difficulty, the strict "rule of law" would not appear to the Americans to be the best method controlling official abuse in cases of this kind: it would either take away all legal methods of dealing with the problem (as was the case in Germany) or would give too much discretion to the investigating officials. At best, the law may explicitly authorize a discretionary solution, but attempt to prevent abuse by submitting the actions of the officials in charge to some independent supervision, say, by requiring officials to obtain a court order in advance of installing a listening device. (Note that this last method also proceeds by vesting a government official, this time the judge, with broad discretion to decide whether the official action is justified by the circumstances.) But even in the absence of any explicit statutory exemption, I am quite sure that all the applicable laws, including the constitutional principles of privacy and freedom from searches and seizures, would be interpreted flexibly enough to allow for a legal installation of listening devices in situations such as this one, and that no official would have to face the burden of violating the law in order to do what it is clearly his duty to do. And this would not be the case because the American law is in any sense "better" than the German, but because the American system would allow that the limits of the rule of law may be narrower than in Germany and that certain official actions, while not specifically controlled by any particular legal provision, may nevertheless be circumscribed by other means, and ultimately "fair" and legitimate.

A similar difference of attitudes can be seen in the broader difference of approaches to the general problem of emergency in the German and American constitutional law systems. War, a state of prolonged crisis, domestic rebellions, and other threats to public order may require extraordinary measures in which respect for individual rights might have to be more than normally subordinated to the claims of public security. A serious problem for every liberal democratic constitution is thus to provide for a strong defense of the rights of individuals, without at the same time crippling the constitutional system itself and making it incapable of dealing with extraordinary situations. The German Constitution provides one model of dealing with this problem, by specifying how and when normal constitutional freedoms can be abridged by the introduction of a well-defined state of emergency. There are clear advantages to this solution: First, no claims of emergency can be made in normal times, since the extraordinary emergency powers can be invoked only in a very formal fashion, requiring parliamentary action. Second, even during a state of emergency, the powers of the government are not unlimited, but clearly prescribed by appropriate constitutional provisions. But the German solution also has its disadvantages. The most serious among them is the very idea of an institutional state of emergency, a state during which normal constitutional protection of individual rights no longer bind the powers that be, and during which extraordinary actions of the authorities are explicitly sanctioned by the highest law of the land. The very fact of allowing such a situation diminishes any power that the law may otherwise have for the protection of the democratic system and of the citizens who are likely to suffer from governmental abuse. Furthermore, the very possibility of a state of emergency may be thought to invite it, to make it less unthinkable, more "normal," and ultimately, as happened in the last years of the Weimar Republic, routine.

The American solution (if it may be so called) to the same problem is not to mention it on the face of the basic law at all, or nearly so. The U.S. Constitution does not have any provisions authorizing the introduction of a formal state of emergency. It does have a provision concerning the introduction of a state of war, but its purpose is clearly to distribute an important foreign relations power between the President and the Congress; while the provision thus has some significance in terms of separation of powers, there is nothing in the document to explain its effect on individual rights. The only indication that emergencies may have some such effect is the statement that the privilege of *habeas corpus* shall not be suspended, except during a war or a rebellion.

Does this mean that under the U.S. Constitution, all the other usual protections of individual rights, as well as all the other institutional safeguards of freedom, such as separation of powers and federalism, remain unaffected by national emergencies? In a way, the answer is yes: with the exception of the writ of *habeas corpus*, no rights can be formally suspended. On the other hand, however, implicit in the document as a whole is the assumption that the Constitution contains no absolutes, i.e., that all Constitutional provisions, including those concerning even the most basic individual rights, must be interpreted with sufficient flexibility to allow for a vindication of paramount national interests. Freedom of speech, for example, can never be "suspended" in an emergency; it simply means something else in such a situation.

In practice, then, the American guarantees of individual liberties, as well as the integrity of the political system as a whole, rely much less than in Germany on purely legal restraints, in the sense of general principles specifying clear limits of governmental actions, and much more on "procedural" arrangements in which particular actors in the governmental bureaucracy might be endowed with a large amount of leeway concerning the substance of their actions, provided they are able to convince other independent (and often competing) actors in the same bureaucracy that these actions are truly indispensable for the achievement of important national objectives.

Again, I do not want to claim that the American way of dealing with the problem of national emergencies is better or worse than the German in the abstract. The choice between them must depend instead on a number of conditions that are likely to differ in any two countries. For the Germans the rule of law may have much greater emotional significance than for the Americans. While the judiciary in the American system may be more easily relied upon to assert its discretionary judgment against the legislature or the executive, the German bureaucracy is more hierarchically structured and the method of pitting various offices against one another may be more difficult to arrange than in a system in which the idea of separation of powers is as deeply rooted as in America. Finally, in a country in which genuine democratic traditions have been historically weaker than the authoritarian or even totalitarian ones, clear legal restraints may look more promising than bureaucratic self-restraint.

Lest it be thought that the preference for discretionary solutions is always stronger in America than on the continent of Europe, we should note a number of cases in which the opposite tendency may be observed, particularly when reliance on experts is concerned. In recent decades, we have seen in America the enormous growth of so called "administrative agencies," which employ large staffs of experts engaged in extensive regulation of private activities. While this regulation is subject to some judicial supervision, the latter usually recognizes the agencies' superior expertise and their discretionary powers, limiting judicial review to cases of the abuse of recognized official discretion. But despite this rapid growth, the "government by experts" is much more recent and of much more modest dimensions in America than in many countries of Europe. To see this, it is enough to move from the federal to the state and local level. To be sure, the federal government has been growing very fast in the United States, but the amount of regulation done at the local level is still very considerable, in fact much more considerable than in most other countries. On this level, however, of necessity, reliance on experts is much more limited. Consider, for example, the case of land use planning, which is nearly completely done by local authorities in the United States, with only minimal interference from the states and nearly none from the federal government. The idea that an average American township can employ genuine experts (urban planners, architects, economists, etc.) in order to optimize the use of its land is obviously impractical. Local officials are usually part-timers, most often elected or recruited according to political rather than professional criteria. The funds from which they are paid are all locally raised and locally controlled, and the share of them that an average community is prepared to spend on regulation of this sort is severely limited. But precisely because local administrators are neither expert nonprofessional civil servants, the likelihood of official abuse is quite high. To control it, official discretion must be narrowly circumscribed by clear legal norms, so that an aggrieved citizen can easily recognize his rights and, if need be, vindicate them in court. As a result, American land-use planning (if such it may be called) is, with the exception of a few large cities, done with the help of a rather crude zoning scheme, imposing a number of restrictions on the types of uses allowable in each area. The fact that regulation is mostly restrictive in character is quite significant here: unlike bans on certain types of construction, an imposition of a particular land-use plan requires confidence in the ability of officials to make difficult concrete decisions of a managerial or aesthetic nature; decisions which, by their very nature, cannot be reduced to a few rules that could, in turn, be judicially enforced. For this reason, such questions as aesthetic regulation have always seemed very problematic in American land-use law: they were always suspected to aim at surreptitious forms of discriminatory exclusion or at best to result in governmental enforced architectural mediocrity.

Anyone who has taken even a short trip through France, Germany, or Italy can immediately observe that the very physiognomy of European landscape is incompatible with the form of land use regulation prevalent in the United States. Towns and villages are more compact, architecturally uniform throughout not just one locality but the entire regions, with different uses mixed together to form full-fledged communities from a cultural as well as an economic point of view. "Zoning" is a term quite inapplicable to the means by which this situation is controlled; land use planning is a field all of its own. Indeed, I was surprised to find that lawyers, as a rule, do not know anything about it, because the field is occupied by architects, urban planners, economists, and other specialists within the state bureaucracy. Litigation about the area is rare and relatively unimportant, precisely because most decisions are integrated into a comprehensive plan of conservation and development in which any particular decision depends on a number of strategic choices, and cannot be questioned in an *ad hoc* manner. Lawyers are thus largely incompetent to judge not only the merits of the plan as a whole, but also of most particular decisions which, by and large, impose concrete solutions on private parties, and leave little room for disagreement.

As in the previous examples, I do not intend to pass judgment as to which solution is "better," but only to compare them at a descriptive level. Clearly, the European model constrains the behavior of private parties to a much greater extent than the American one. On the other hand, precisely because the decisions made in the European model do not have to be translated into the language of legal norms, certain aims which are very difficult to achieve through legal means (such as aesthetic quality, for example, which might be relatively objectively judged by competent persons, but can hardly be expressed in terms of general rules) are much better pursued in the European system. And finally, the sheer logistic problems of running a competent bureaucracy capable of advanced land use planning may be at odds with a far reaching American-type decentralization of state administrative machinery.

I could multiply these examples (and one could probably question the accuracy of those I already gave), but my point is either already made or cannot be made at all. The rule of law is a very good thing, but its genuine function is often obscured by an abstract philosophical perspective which makes it more difficult to see its inherent limitations. In fact, not only is the scope of the validity of this worthy principle somewhat narrower than is usually believed, but its meaning is often distorted: instead of being an element of external control of bureaucratic abuse, the rule of law is in fact an inherently bureaucratic device of administrative self control and it very much relies on bureaucracy for its effectiveness. Moreover, it is only one of a number of such devices, and a decision as to whether or not it should be used should always be weighed against the costs and benefits of using some discretionary alternatives.

•

FIVE

THE IDEA AND PRACTICE OF LIBERAL DEMOCRACY AND THE MODERN UNIVERSITY, WITH SOME COMMENTS ON THE MODERN PRIVATE UNIVERSITY

Edward Shils

The relations between liberal democratic societies and universities have come in the twentieth century to be continuous, very demanding from both sides, intense and not always harmonious. It has not always been that way. They were once more sporadic, more separate from each other. Much more is demanded of universities than ever before; the universities are expected to do things for society which were not previously expected of it. On the other side, the universities are more demanding on financial resources from society and particularly from government. The universities are called upon by their societies to lend a helping hand more frequently and even when they are not called upon to intervene, they frequently do so on their own initiative.

It is now said that universities are indispensable to the purposes of a democratic society. Many university teachers regard universities as bulwarks of liberalism, meaning in most cases, collectivistic liberalism. Universities are on ceremonial occasions proclaimed as "bulwarks of a free society." Sometimes the universities were viewed as alien to democracy if not to liberalism.

The traditions of the European Enlightenment of the seventeenth to the nineteenth centuries were not brought to bear on universities until much later. It cannot be said that Bacon's scientistic ideas had any influence on the attitudes or the policies of British and French universities towards scientific research in the seventeenth and eighteenth centuries. The French encyclopedists had no interest in the furtherance of their ideas through universities and certainly not through the French universities which they despised. Although in the twentieth century, American universities and most recently administrators of British and German universities have followed policies which look very Baconian, their predecessors of two centuries ago certainly did not share their views.

The first sorties of liberal and democratic ideas, as far as they were from the theories which later became associated with the liberal democratic kind of society, were nevertheless foreshadowing of some of the ideas which went into the practice of universities and into the attitudes toward them. These ideas were not directly influential in the formation of the universities of their time. What is now thought to be a distinctive feature of the free university in liberal democratic societies was its creation by societies which were neither liberal nor democratic.

The Inheritance of the Pre-Liberal Age

Universities may be regarded as part of the inheritance for which modern liberal democratic societies are indebted to the

Middle Ages. The idea and the scattered reality of autonomous institutions devoted to the training of young persons in the most advanced knowledge of their time and to the cultivation and even occasionally the making of a further advancement in that knowledge were the greatest gift of the Middle Ages to modern times. Christian belief and its church and less prominently Jewish belief and Roman law were themselves gifts of antiquity to the Middle Ages which then transmitted to them in variously modified forms to modern times. The university in contrast was a genuine institutional creation of an age thought too retrograde in matters of invention. The autonomous university as a corporate body for the teaching and cultivation of the most advanced and ordered knowledge was perhaps the greatest institutional creation of the European Middle Ages and with the great works of medieval art, architecture, it remains the most appreciated. The modern forms of the medieval Christian church and Christian theology have now been exceeded by the universities.

The universities were inherited by Western liberal democratic societies from medieval and early modern societies which were neither democratic nor liberal. Even when the universities began to come down to their present form in the nineteenth century, some of the societies in which they were created and flourished greatly were neither liberal nor democratic. Nevertheless, it cannot be said that even in the first half of the nineteenth century there were no significant interconnections between universities and liberalism and democracy. Some of the ideas which entered into the formation of universities, although not avowedly liberal when they first appeared (the very word in its recent senses did not even exist), were later assimilated into the constitution of liberalism. The preliberal ideas and institutional forms are now regarded as integral to liberal society and to the universities which are now thought to be indispensable to liberal democracy. Such is the "cunning of reason"! (*List der Vernunft.*)

THE BALANCE OF FREEDOM

The Heritage of Autonomy: The autonomy of universities as communities of teachers and scholars, was, in fact, established in the first centuries of their existence in the twelfth and thirteenth centuries. It has since become an essential feature of the literal conception of the university. It was certainly not the outcome of a liberal outlook in the present sense of the word. It came partly from the "feudal idea of liberty," i.e., the freedom of corporate bodies like estates, guilds and municipalities, partly it was a beneficiary of the conflicts between the papacy, earthly territorial sovereigns and municipal authorities. The university was a corporate body, made up by its teachers and students. Its members enjoyed certain legal privileges in consequence of their membership in the university.

The Heritage of the Pursuit of Truth: The appreciation of the dignity of the pursuit of truth which at present appears to be essential to a free or liberal, and nowadays a liberal-democratic, society was not until fairly recent times regarded as related to the freedom of action of individuals, or to any belief that the free pursuit of truth was necessary to the goodness of a society or its satisfactory working. The individual's right to unhampered enquiry and to the free publication of the results of enquiry were not among the legitimation which accompanied the academic pursuit of learning in the sixteenth and seventeenth centuries. But the pursuit of truth, the belief that it was the responsibility of the university to transmit truths they regarded as important was the foundation of universities in the preliberal age, as much as it has ever been in the past two centuries. Although it is true that it was only in the nineteenth century that universities began to produce scientific and scholarly works on a large scale, the practice of science and scholarship were both well established in the everyday life of universities in the seventeenth and eighteenth centuries. The universities of Leyden, Utrecht, Halle, etc. were outstanding in their time and ever since. They established the pattern which came fully into flower in the nineteenth century.

Although the professional faculties in the universities taught techniques, the universities were not regarded as institutions for technical training alone. They were supposed to teach the fundamental truths of these subjects.

The Heritage of External Patronage: Another feature of universities in Great Britain and the United States in the nineteenth and twentieth centuries has been patronage by possessors of wealth other than governments; this helped to sustain the autonomy of universities *vis-à-vis* government. There is nothing modern about that; it was practiced long before liberal-democratic societies came into existence. The two ancient universities of Great Britain, Oxford and Cambridge, were private in the sense of being nongovernmental institutions in initiation, financial support and control. The first American colleges of the Colonial period were also private institutions, supported by gifts from nongovernmental patrons—and from fees paid by students.

The use of the term "private" in this context is negative. It signifies only an institution nongovernmental in initiation, support and control. Within the category of the nongovernmental, there were ecclesiastically chartered, supported and controlled universities and colleges and those which were supported by the laity, although often for religious purposes. There were combinations of privacy in support and ecclesiastical control. Universities with lay governing bodies and with support by private nonecclesiastical patrons were unknown until the nineteenth century in Great Britain where the "modern universities" were of that sort and some American colleges and universities.

These modes of support were neither liberal nor democratic although some of them became characteristic of liberal democratic societies. In the twentieth century, the gifts conferred by large private philanthropic foundations and the wealthy private philanthropists became significant bulwarks of the autonomy of universities in the face of government, thus helping to maintain what had, in the meantime, become an important institutional feature of the liberal-democratic society, namely, the autonomy of the university in a pluralistic society.

There are other features which are characteristic of universities prior to the age of liberal democracy. Among the most important of these were the systems of examinations covering delimited subjects and the award of degrees. Similarly, the lecture as a device of instruction is an inheritance from the premodern university. The degrees still retain the pattern of the past. In ceremonial matters, universities still continue the models of their preliberal existence. Academic gowns and academic titles of rank and authority still persist.

The relations of the universities to liberal democracy are illustrative of how a tradition generated in one context, or rather in one setting of traditions, persists and becomes relatively harmonious with another, quite different setting of traditions.

Of course, both the liberal and the democratic strands of the liberal democratic tradition itself have existed since antiquity. They did not come together in their present, not easily maintained, collaboration until very many centuries later, after long and intricate elaborations. For most of this long period of nearly two millennia, neither had anything to do with universities. Here and there, these anticipatory traditions touched or were touched by the universities. For example, the cultivation of Roman law in the twelfth century in Bologna could be looked upon as an anticipation of the liberal ideas of law as a rational intellectual subject and of the supremacy of law over the arbitrary command of the prince. Nevertheless, it was not in its time thought to have anything to do with the complex patterns of belief which were later called liberalism and liberal democracy.

DEMOCRACY AND THE MODERN UNIVERSITY

I

The First Stirrings of Liberalism and the Universities in their Reciprocal Relations

The American universities and the American colleges which later became universities, e.g., Harvard, Columbia, Yale, Princeton, unlike the great European universities, were all founded in a time when what we now call liberal ideas were being much discussed by philosophers and publicists. Nevertheless, the ideas which presided over the founding of American universities and colleges in the earliest years of the nineteenth century were not the ideas of liberal democracy. The private colleges which were established before the American Revolution and the formation of the United States were not intended to serve a liberal democracy. They were intended to instruct young men who would enter the clergy or who might play a part of significance in oligarchical colonial societies. Neither in their course of study, nor in their policy of recruitment nor in the careers toward which they sought to suit the youths who were under their care, did they think of a democratic society as the setting of their subsequent careers. There was no expectation that colleges and universities would educate a large part of the generation between the ages of 15 and 20 nor was there any intention that the institutions of higher education in the colonial period would take their places as exemplars or broadcasters of liberal ideals. There certainly was no notion that they would enable their graduates to contribute to the material wealth of their society. Fragmentary approximations began to appear in the eighteenth century. The universities and colleges of the newly independent United States offered curricula which were much influenced by the undergraduate courses of study at the ancient British universities, teaching mainly mathematics and classics. They drew no inspiration from the study of the Latin and Greek classics for the training of citizens of a liberal society. It is true that the "founding fathers" knew something of classic political philosophy and history and they also knew about the history of republican city states, but such matters were not prominent in higher education. It was only later in the nineteenth century when these subjects were appraised in Great Britain as the right ones for the education of the minds of higher civil servants that the universities were brought into positive connection with the first striving of a rationally ordered liberal society.

The American colleges and universities early in the nineteenth century began to introduce subjects drawn from the Scottish universities—moral philosophy and political economy. In this way they were affected by the Scottish Enlightenment and with the formative ideas of liberalism. The first opening of American higher education to liberal ideas came with the establishment of the University of Virginia by Thomas Jefferson. (Jefferson had recruited and appointed teachers from Scotland. Some of these later returned to University College London, thus bringing to London Scottish ideas about higher education admixed with Jeffersonian liberal rationalism.) The writings of Adam Smith began to appear in the syllabuses of the American colleges and universities. With that came a breath of European liberalism in its beginnings.

Liberal Skepticism about Universities

The liberal thinkers did not have an especially high opinion of universities nor did they think that they had any great part to play in liberal society. In Western Europe, neither Tocqueville nor Constant thought seriously about universities and they had no great expectations that they would contribute much to the effective operation of free institutions. Adam Smith had a rather low opinion of universities and university teachers, although he was a university teacher for a great part of his life. He surely did not regard universities as the intellectual engines of liberal society. John Stuart Mill did not expect any great help for liberalism or democracy from universities. (Humboldt's ideas about the *Grenzen der Wirksamkeit des Staates*, were taken up in part by John Stuart Mill in his *Essay on Liberty* as were his ideas on individuality and character in their relation to liberty, but not his ideas about universities.)

Idealistic Liberalism

The German Contribution: there was one great European liberal of the early nineteenth century who for a short time interested himself in universities. That was Wilhelm von Humboldt. He was the first great point where European liberalism touched on universities. His effect transformed the universities of Prussia and then of the world.

The belief in the formation of the character of cultivated autonomous individuals was the product of idealistic German philosophical thought. Fichte's idea of "the calling of the scholar" could be said to be a liberal idea but it did not envisage the individual as a citizen in a liberal society as much as it did the individual as an end in himself. Freedom was necessary for the development of character, of a harmonious whole within the individual, rather than as a condition which would enable the individual to pursue his own freely chosen ends by the use of his own reasoning powers and his own cognitive assessment of the situation of his action.

The first influence of liberalism in European universities occurred with von Humboldt's memorandum on "the state of our learned institutions" from which emerged the University of Berlin. The liberalism which was expressed in the memorandum was the idealistic liberalism which looked to the universities for the formation of the autonomous cultivated character. The ideals of the unity of research and teaching (*Einheit der Forschung und Lehre*), the freedom of teaching and learning (*Freiheit der Lehre und des Lernens*) and of academic self-government (*akademische Selbstverwaltuno*) which developed in German thought about universities in the first half of the nineteenth century were liberal ideals but they were not products of the individualistic liberalism of British provenance; von Humboldt did not think of the practical utility of what is discovered and taught in universities, although he did take it for granted that they would produce higher civil servants educated in law. Nor did he think of universities as providing the training for civility in the leadership of society. The highest good to which universities would contribute was the formation of individuality or character and the means to this was the disciplined, methodical search for truth through free and unhampered research. From this emerged the ideal of academic freedom which then became an integral feature of universities of many countries in the nineteenth century, not least of those with quite a different tradition of liberalism. It is not suggested that ideal of academic freedom was exclusively a product of German idealism. It arose in part from the experience of an academic profession, increasingly acquiring an academic collective self-consciousness, confronted by the repressive actions of governments, churches and influential private individuals.

Academic Freedom

Humboldtian and Benthamite Liberalism: The academic freedom which became a major part of the program and constitution of the German university was a different sort of thing from what academic freedom became much later in the United States. It began with the intention of fostering the morally autonomous character. For that, the freedoms of teaching and research were necessary. It also required the civil or political freedom but that was not an end; only a means. The justification for the political freedom of the academic later became a most important element in the argument for academic freedom when that ideal began to be discussed in American universities in the last two decades of the nineteenth century and throughout the twentieth century. This was not the case in Germany where academic freedom was required for the fulfillment of individuality. In America it was regarded as a requirement for the discovery and the teaching of scientific and scholarly truth as an end in itself and also a precondition for the rational pursuit of ends in society. This

116

was a significant change in part of the substance of a tradition consequent in the shift from idealistic to rational-individualistic liberalism.

The foundation of University College London was also another point where liberalism, individualistic and utilitarian liberalism, and the universities came together. This institution was founded by the liberal utilitarians led by George Grote, the historian of Greek liberty—under the inspiration of Jeremy Bentham. One of the main intentions of the founding Benthamites was to offer higher education for offspring of the professional and business classes at lower cost than at Oxford and Cambridge. By aiming to serve the middle class, it widened the range from which its students came. It was in this respect a forerunner of the democratization of universities. Insofar as it was the intention of liberalism to extend participation in public life to the middle and lower classes, then the foundation of University College London by easy attendance of the middle classes, could be said to have been a step in the direction of the liberal society. But the intention was certainly not explicit.

University College London became the first institution of higher education in the English-speaking world to cultivate the full range of modern academic subjects and to devote itself assiduously to research and to offer training in research. In this respect, it was the forerunner of those universities which have come to be regarded as essential institutions of liberal democracy. University College London was a liberal institution also in the sense that it deliberately refused to have any requirements of subscription to any church or religious belief as a condition of admission as a student or appointment as a teacher. Its development was parallel to and in frequent contact with the German universities as they were developing in the nineteenth century under the influence of von Humboldt's liberal ideals and of the University of Berlin which embodied those ideals.

II
Liberalism and More Complex Interactions between Universities

Germany: A complex affinity between universities and liberalism began to emerge in the nineteenth century. As the universities became more productive in scientific research, a scientistic skepticism about tradition and religion became more prominent in universities. University teachers became participants in the organs of public opinion and they also came more frequently—not very frequently however—into conflict with the authorities of church and particularly the state. In consequence, demands of academic freedom came more to the fore as did criticisms of authority for restricting it. These were all very incipient tendencies, still very rare but clearly evident in retrospect. They all moved in the direction of a link between universities and liberalism. It should be emphasized however that these developments still occupied only a very small place in the world of universities.

The German academic profession in the first half of the nineteenth century was not only permeated by the liberal ideals of the freedom of research and teachings, it was also liberal in its public political activities. The liberalism of the "Gottingen Seven" who were dismissed for their criticism of the unconstitutional activities of the kind of Hanover in 1837 lived on in the German revolution of 1848, when in the liberal parliament meeting in Frankfurt, about one third of the deputies were university professors. By the time of the formation of the German Empire in 1871, political liberalism faded from the German academic profession but the ideals of the unity of research and teaching, of the freedom of teaching and study, and of academic self-government did not fade. They persisted undiminished. Nor did devotion to the *Rechtsstaat*. Even in the period of the Weimar Republic, when many German professors were politically conservative and hostile to the liberal-democratic republic, those particular ideals remained largely unimpaired.

So strong was the conviction of the dignity of scientific and scholarly knowledge that any departure from its standards was deplored and resisted. There were limits on the consistency with which this conviction was observed. Before the First World War, socialists were not looked upon as fit to teach in a German university. Jews, too, were disfavored when it came to university appointments except in the medical faculty, although there was anti-Semitism there too. There were genuinely liberal professors who tried to undo this limitation on the primacy of strictly intellectual standards but they were often unsuccessful. The situation in these respects changed under the Weimar Republic, but at the end of that period the German universities lost nearly all the virtues which they had acquired from universities of the age of absolutism and humanism and princely states and from the humanistic liberalism of the neoclassical period. During this time which ran for more than a century, the German universities maintained certain features which although not liberal in origin, became part of the liberal tradition.

German academic liberalism took for granted the centrality of the state. It was therefore consistent that in matters of economic policy, German academics were collectivistic, however much they disliked socialism.

It should be pointed out that the German universities at the height of their devotion to academic freedom never questioned that they were "institutions of the state," and that the government retained the final and definitive decision regarding appointments and the establishment of new subjects and new chairs. It was accepted by academics that the promulgation of the statutes and bylaws of the university was a prerogative of the government, not merely approved and enacted but also promulgated by the government. In comparison with the situation of American and British universities the autonomy of the German university was relatively restricted and these restrictions were accepted. But these restrictions very seldom intruded into the freedom of teaching and research of a teacher once appointed. The cases of infringement of academic freedom in Germany were invariably infringements on the civil freedom of academics. One case is that of Theodore Lessing, a teacher of history at a technological college. Two cases of infringement on the civil freedom of academics involved *Privatdozenten* whose appointments were legally not under governmental jurisdiction at all; these were the cases in the 1920s of Ernst J. Gumbel, a statistician, and of Leo Arons, a physicist, in the 1890s.

France. The French universities did not exist as corporate bodies until well into the nineteenth century. What was called the *Universite de France* was the name of the entire system of higher educational facilities and the system of secondary schools. The faculties had no relationship with each other, administratively, by proximity or by common name. There was no university autonomy.

The "real" higher educational system of France consisted of the *grandes ecoles*, a set of specialized professional training institutions, several of which became outstanding for their scholarly and scientific achievements in research and their high level of teaching. These institutions were branches of the various ministries to which their subjects were particularly pertinent. Autonomy did not exist for these institutions in any legal sense. Several of them developed a high degree of *espirit de corps*, at least among their students and alumni.

The *grandes ecoles* were favored institutions which operated at a high intellectual level; they were intended to prepare intellectually outstanding men, for the civil service, for the technological departments of government and for teaching in secondary schools. These great intellectual institutions were to some extent continuations of the traditions of the absolutist regime which were inimical to corporate autonomy.

The French universities thus did not enjoy the prerogatives conferred by liberalism. They progressed toward the freedom of research and teaching only very slowly and toward autonomy even more slowly. For much of the nineteenth century, the central ministerial authorities—French educational administration was very centralized—sought to discourage teachers in the provinces from doing research. University teachers who expressed political opinions distasteful to the government were dismissed. Instances of such treatment were not infrequent.

Perhaps in response to these indignities, French academics in the second half of the nineteenth century became more and more demanding of academic freedom. Thus, whatever might have been the case among French academics previously, liberal attitudes became more common among them by the latter part of the century. When, in 1893, almost a hundred intellectuals signed the letter drafted by Emile Zola—*J'accuse*—in defense of Captain Dreyfus, for publication in *l'Aurore*, about one third were academics, mainly in humanistic disciplines (including the social sciences). I think that only one academic was among the public supporters of the government for its condemnation of Dreyfus and its refusal to reopen the case. The attitude of the academic, as well as the literary signatories of "*J'accuse*" was clearly a liberal one. It was an attitude which demanded equality before the law, religious toleration, equality of opportunity ("career open to talents"), free scrutiny of governmental actions, the appreciation of the power of pubic opinion, etc. All of these are among the primary and derivative articles of liberal belief. There were undoubtedly conservatives and reactionaries in the Sorbonne, the *ecole normale superieure* and the *ecole pratique les hautes etudes*, but the running was done by the liberals and democrats who around the turn of century were also often socialists. They were secularists, if not anti-clerical. They were in short the embodiment of the academic ethos of the Third Republic. Albert Thibaudet was right to call the Third Republic the *Republique des professeurs*. This was a period of increasing academic freedom inside and outside the universities, i.e., in the content of teaching and research and in the public expression of political attitudes. Although *de facto* autonomy increased in the universities—they became corporate bodies instead of an informal cluster of separate faculties only in 1893—the ministry of education kept a firm and highly centralized control over syllabuses, requirements for degrees, the creation of new chairs and other aspects of university autonomy. The universities, especially the provincial ones, were financially neglected by the government and by the wealthy classes. French scientific activity was marked by outstanding individual achievements but neither the government nor the public did much to promote and increase the scale of that activity by greatly increased support. France was like Germany in the sense that its universities were state - universities. One exception was the *ecole libre des sciences politiques* founded in 1872 in response to the defeat by Prussia in the war of 1870-1871, by private initiative (Emile Boutmy) and by private financial support (the Duchess de Galliera); the other was the Institut Catholique founded in 1875.

The United States: In the United States, collective liberalism gained ground among university teachers from the last part of the nineteenth century, although the majority, especially in natural scientific, technological and professional subjects did not share in the collective liberal view. As the university teachers became more liberal in the collectivistic sense, so did the university become a more liberal institution in a more liberal society. The establishment of the elective system and the greater diversity of courses of study in the education of undergraduates increasingly displaced the fixed and narrow curriculum of the earlier period. Religious qualifications within the universities of Protestant foundation for academic appointments were less frequently invoked. Jews and Roman Catholics continued, however, until the end of the period between the two world wars, to be considered very charily. Until the 1930s, Negroes were never appointed outside predominantly or exclusively Negro universities and colleges; when the situation changed in that decade, it changed only very slightly. It is not that there were many aspirants among the Roman Catholics and Negroes. Jews on the other hand were available in large numbers but until the 1930s, they, too, were seldom appointed in most universities, and often with reluctance and even against opposition.

This increased openness of the universities was a function of the improvement of the academic ethos in American universities as they improved in the intellectual achievements of their teaching staffs. Nevertheless, academic freedom, in the sense of the civil freedom of academics, was occasionally sharply reproved. There were many cases of the infringement of the civil freedom of academics and this in turn heightened the demand by academics for their protection from such infringements. Between the two world wars and, again, after the Second World War, there were a number of investigations by legislative bodies, federal and state, into allegedly subversive organizations and activities, and university teachers sometimes came within their purview, resulting in embarrassment in many cases and in dismissal in a small number. In the late 1940s and 1950s, the state legislature of California demanded that teachers swore on oath an affirmation of the loyalty to the United States Constitution. Since in the United States, even in state universities, teachers do not have the legal status of the civil servants, this was an infringement on university autonomy. On the whole, despite these often irrational attacks on universities, the autonomy of the universities was sustained.

Changes in the status of universities occurred *pari passu* with the forward movement of the idea of a liberal democratic society. As societies became more liberal democratic, the more universities came under the jurisdiction of that ideal.

State and Private Universities: In the United States, when the new republic launched itself on its career, state universities were formed mainly in the states (recently colonies) in which there were no already established and dominant private colleges. (For example, Massachusetts, Connecticut, New Jersey and New York had no state universities until very recently since they already had Harvard College, Yale College,

Princeton University and Columbia College (called King's College during the colonial period). The first state universities were formed in the southern seaboard states which had no significant privately founded and supported colleges. Private colleges and universities continued to be created in the United States throughout the nineteenth century, even in states which had state universities. In Great Britain, the major modern universities—Manchester, Birmingham, Leeds and Liverpool—were founded by private initiative and they were also supported almost entirely by private patronage. Even now private patronage is very important to American colleges and universities and even to some of the leading state universities.

Liberal-democratic societies are pluralistic societies; voluntary associations and free corporate bodies, privately founded and conducted are parts of their constitutions. Yet the independent private creation of a university has, with the exceptions of the United States and Great Britain and territories which were once parts of the British Empire, been very rare. The *Universite libre de Bruxelles* founded in 1834, the *Vrije Universiteit* of Amsterdam founded in 1880, the *Liberal Universite di Economia e Commercio "Luigi Bocconi"* of Milan founded in 1902 have probably had, as far as I know, no followers in their footsteps until the University College of Buckingham (now the University of Buckingham since 1983) founded in 1973, and several private institutions in Western Germany.

Roman Catholic universities are interesting in this context. By definition their autonomy is restricted by the obligation to maintain the Roman Catholic faith. Many of them have renounced this requirement for appointment in all faculties except the theological faculty. (The German state universities, by the Concordat, maintain this qualification for appointment to chairs in Roman Catholic theology, which must have episcopal approval. But this restriction of academic autonomy is well accepted in the requirement that the ultimate decision regarding all professional appointment rests with the state Ministry of education.)

124

The Intended Function of Universities in the Liberal Age

The Fusion of Ordered Knowledge into Society: One motive for establishment and expansion of universities in the United States was an aspiration to realize one of the ideals of liberalism, namely, to introduce rationality and soundly based knowledge into the management of the affairs of society. Another closely related motive for the establishment of universities and colleges in the United States, both private and public, was respect for the spiritual sphere and an acknowledgement that a society must make provision for the cultivation of the spiritual sphere; one closely related motive is the desire of the church for an educated clergy. These attitudes long antedate the origins of liberal society. (In the Middle Ages, the Church was the predominant object of such respect and acknowledgement; universities in time began to share that position.) Another motive of increasing importance in the late Middle Ages and early modern times was the desire of rulers for trained officials who would free them from dependence on aristocratic families and who would be loyal and relatively rational administrators of the royal will. Universities in time came to share the status of the church, as the liberal democratic societies became more secular, the universities came to have a higher standing than the churches. Still, the functions for which universities were founded remained much the same. The spiritual sphere was gradually reinterpreted as the cultural sphere. The professional training function of the university expanded greatly in proportion to the spirited—later cultural—functions. Liberalism gave prominence to the function of universities to provide rational-empirical knowledge for the guidance of conduct of affairs in society. The new function was a fusion of the cultural and training function. More scientifically oriented than the provision for the spiritual and later cultural functions, less empirical and less concerned with technical recipes than the training function, the universities acquired a new function in the nineteenth century, namely, the provision of fundamental knowledge methodically acquired and ordered by principle or theory for the dual tasks of illuminating the human mind and providing rationality and scientific knowledge for those who are to exercise authority in society. Thus the functions of the university of the Middle Ages were reinterpreted to the satisfaction of the liberal ideals of individual rationality and a society infused with rational scientific knowledge.

The belief in the value of reason and sound, methodically acquired empirical knowledge for society had been given a vivid presentation by Francis Bacon in *The New Atlantis*, at the threshold of modern times. English liberalism, in the form of the Benthamite maxim of "Investigate, agitate, legislate," did not reach the universities of its home country for a long time, but in Scotland, Adam Smith's and Adam Ferguson's teaching and writing represented a step in that direction. It was, oddly enough, in Germany where the Baconian and Benthamite beliefs in rational statecraft were philosophically repugnant, that the idea of the guidance of government through social enquiry had a firm footing in the universities which had been given the task of training young men for the civil service, including a rather primitive kind of economics as part of the legal training required for appointment to the civil service. German academic economics had a principled insistence on descriptive empirical research. This tradition led to the establishment of the *Verein für Sozialpolitik*. This organization with its steady flow of meticulously documented monographs on the economic and social problems of German society had a firm footing in the universities, many of its most active members being academics. Germany was at that time a less liberal and less democratic society than Great Britain, yet it was in Germany that the specifically liberal idea of empirical social enquiry as a means of illuminating public opinion and hereby guiding government settled in the universities. Great Britain had such investigations, but they had no connection with universities until well into the twentieth century. The second society to take the social sciences into its universities was American society.

Universities in the United States took to the entire range of the social sciences with much enthusiasm; they went far beyond the German universities in the branches of learning. The movement began in the last quarter of the nineteenth century, first at Johns Hopkins University and then at the University of Chicago on a much larger scale and with a much wider variety. Columbia University was an important center, like Johns Hopkins and Chicago, deriving impetus from the German universities. They gradually spread to the other universities, at first mostly the state universities of the Middle West, and somewhat later the most famous of the older Eastern universities.

The inspiration for this mode of descriptive social investigation—now established as an indispensable part of a liberal democratic society—was first experienced by American academics during their period of study in German universities from the 1870s onwards. American academics saw in the *Verein fur Sozialpolitik* a model for the enlightening influence of social investigation of public and political opinion. This was at the bottom of the teaching of economics at Johns Hopkins University. It was there that American academic collectivistic liberalism first became rooted and from there its seed spread to other American universities. The more traditional individualistic liberalism of British, especially Scottish, political economy also took root in the American universities. The latter kind of liberalism in the universities—mainly in departments of economics—was as interested in influencing governmental policies as was the academic collectivistic liberalism, but it wished to influence them in the opposite direction, namely, the policy of fortifying the workings of the competitive market and of individual enterprise. British economists testified before governmental commissions of enquiry or served on them. American academic economists did the same.

THE BALANCE OF FREEDOM

The foundation of the National Academy of Sciences in 1863 was another of the steps to realize the ideal of the liberal enlightenment by proffering scientific advice to government on the basis of knowledge gained through scientific research; this took place before American universities were producing much of that kind of knowledge. (Nevertheless, two of the moving spirits in the foundation of the Academy at a time when much of American scientific activity was not done in universities were Asa Gray and Louis Agassiz, both of them professors at Harvard University.)

The American universities never attained the preponderance in training for the highest levels of the civil service that was achieved by German universities and by the University of Oxford. One reason why the American universities did not come to the forefront as sources of recruits to the higher civil service was because the "spoils system" remained for a long time the well-entrenched and chief method of recruitment for the civil service. The higher positions in the service just below the cabinet were filled by the incoming party by persons who had become eminent in public life as politicians and as lawyers. Nevertheless, the reform of the civil service at all levels aimed at the recruitment of officials by competitive examinations, to which only persons with a specified amount of education were admitted, was the work of university graduates who had studied in Germany and who had before their minds both the German and the British civil services—the latter after the reform of 1853.

The highest positions in the German civil service had been reserved for graduates of the law faculties of German universities. This practice of drawing upon the universities as institutions to train young persons in rational judgement and technical knowledge for public service is far older than any liberal democratic society. The British reforms both at home and in India were, in contrast with the German practice, the product of Whig and radical liberalism; these reforms intended to replace primordial criteria of recruitment by recruitment on the basis of performance in competitive examination to which admission was restricted to young men with high academic qualifications. The recruitment of highly educated experts for the service of the rulers was originally a policy of absolute monarchy; it later became an article of faith of liberal regimes. The illumination of public opinion by the results of systematic social investigation came somewhat later. If was part of the same intention of infusing ordered knowledge into the functioning of society.

III
Specific Features of Liberal Democratic Societies

After this brief historical sketch of the antecedents' interactions of liberal beliefs in the universities, it is now appropriate to make a more general survey of the way in which particular features of modern liberal democratic societies and universities infringe on each other, for better or for worse.

I will begin by enumerating, unsystematically, some of the features of liberal democratic societies and then I will enquire into how these affect universities and to what extent and in which ways academics have contributed to them.

Modern liberal democratic societies are characterized by:

1) *The Dispersion of Authority*

This involves resistance to the concentration of authority in the central government; it involves dispersion of governmental authority among central, regional and local centers. Liberal democracies require a far-reaching autonomy of institutions in their relations with government and with each other.

Liberal democracy entails individual responsibility and mutual aid independent of central authority.

In recent decades there has been a widespread tendency for the pluralism of voluntary associations to turn into the pluralism of associations to elicit governmental action for the benefit of the participants of the association or third parties. Mutual aid has turned in the direction of the demand for central governmental action.

2)   *Separation de facto of Church from State and Society*

The separation of church and state has resulted from a renunciation of the aspiration of religious bodies to control the entire range of social institutions and from a readiness of government and society to permit all religions to propagate their beliefs, to conduct religious rituals and instruction and to own property. These pluralistic arrangements have been accompanied by the exclusion of religious belief and religious affiliation as criteria affecting admission to universities and to academic appointments, and the far-reaching neutrality of religious bodies with respect to the quest for and transmission of scientific and scholarly knowledge.

3)   *Market Economy*

The competitive market economy, hamstrung by collectivistic liberalism, remains to a very large extent the pattern of economic life of liberal democratic societies. The market presupposes private property. This is now generally accepted in liberal-democratic societies, although the steady advance of collectivistic liberalism and social democracy have restricted the scope of the market economy in the course of the present century. In recent decades, there has been a recovery of the market economy and a retraction of collectivistic liberalism and social democracy.

4)   *The Rule of Law*

The rule of law protects the structure of liberal democracy by opposing the arbitrariness of officials and thereby maintaining the liberties of the citizen. By holding in check the arbitrariness of government, the rule of law strengthens the legitimacy of liberal democratic society; it also encourages the initiative of the individual citizens. The rule of law depends on the determination of the legal profession and of the judiciary selected from that profession to uphold it.

5)   *Representative Institutions*

Representative institutions are the crucial elements of liberal democratic societies. It was from the tradition of representation in antiquity and in the Middle Ages that the pattern of

130

legislative institutions filled through popular elections grew. The extension of the franchise which permitted a wider participation in the selection of representatives, was the heart of democracy; it was the grafting of democracy into liberalism. The idea of representative institutions with two or more parties competing in elections on the basis of a universal adult franchise entails a whole monopoly of institutions through which public opinion is formed and expressed. These fall under the heading of:

6)   *Freedom of Expression of Beliefs*

Freedom of expression of beliefs about all the objects of public and intellectual interest is essential to liberal democracy. Without it liberal democracy does not exist. Freedom of expression includes freedom of enquiry, i.e., in choice of subjects, in the choice of methods of enquiry and in the promulgation of enquiry; it includes the freedom of publication; it entails the rights of individuals to form their own opinion in the evaluation of artistic and literary works.

The foregoing list of features of liberal democratic societies enumerates their institutional components. Here are other features which fall into the sphere of culture or symbolic objectives, i.e., the sphere of knowledge and beliefs, cognitive and normative. These are the following. (The list is not exhaustive or systematic.)

7)   *The Propagation of Ordered Knowledge*

Liberal democracy has from its beginning prized the possession of methodically gained, ordered, empirical knowledge. Liberalism with its emphasis on rationality and in purposeful action has been regarded by its proponents as under obligation to foster the growth and propagation of that kind of knowledge which includes scientific and scholarly knowledge, reliable descriptive knowledge of nature and society, including knowledge of individuals, the accurate reporting or description of current events, including governmental, political and economic activities. This has led to the "specialist" or "expert."

Such knowledge is prized for its own sake, i.e., because it sustains the rational scientifically enlightened mind; it is also prized for its application to practical activities in technology, social institutions, economic life, political and administrative affairs, etc. The high estimation of the value of such knowledge entails widespread access to such knowledge through education, publication, the restriction of the scope of secrecy, especially regarding the activities of governments.

8)   *Commensurations of Rewards with Achievement*

The superiority of individual achievement as a claim to preferment, over the criteria of birth, religion, race, etc., is one of the major features of modern liberal-democratic societies. This has many sources. One of them is the metaphysical-moral belief in the value of the individual as an intrinsically valuable entity; it has gradually gained the upper hand over status derived from lineage and role within the family. It is this which has distinguished liberal-democratic societies from tribal, feudal, aristocratic oligarchical and totalitarian societies.

This entails the opening of appointments to occupational and professional posts in accordance with past achievements and with a view to expected performance in the future. ("Careers open to talents"). It also entails a high appreciation of specialized expertise. This in turn implies a high appreciation of highly specialized training and of highly specialized professional careers. Liberalism appreciates equality of opportunity. Liberalism does not in principle appreciate "equality of results." In recent decades in Western liberal democratic countries there has been a demand for policies promoting "equality of results." This is contrary to the principles of liberal democracy. There has simultaneously been much hostility against "elitism" which means discrimination of assessment of works of art and literature, against the criterion of achievement and prospective achievement in appointments and against rewards proportionate to achievement. All these demands are contrary to the principle of liberal democracy.

132

9) *Humanitarianism*

Humanitarianism is solicitude for the peripheries of society, e.g., the Lumpenproletarian, homeless persons, outcasts of all sorts, women, children, the unemployed, and impoverished. Humanitarianism is not integral in principle to either liberalism or democracy. It was not appreciated by socialism or communism. However, it has come to be part of the program of liberal democracy and its deformed variant collectivistic liberalism.

10) *Efficiency and Rationalization*

Liberalism, being oriented towards rationality attributes values to "efficiency" in the expenditure of resources, time and energy, etc. Liberal society, oriented toward the market, is concerned with the economic adaptation of scarce resources to alternative ends. This rests on calculation of costs and benefits.

This is one aspect of the rationalization of liberal democratic societies; this has already been touched on in the remarks above under "specialized expertise," professional training, the appreciation of the scientific approach to the understanding and management of society, etc.

11) *Disparagement of Primordial Institutions, Tradition and Traditionality*

A major tradition of liberalism is the disparagement of primordial institutions (families, nations, etc.), of traditions and traditionality which it regards as irrational or superstitious. This is perhaps the chief point of disagreement between conservatism and liberal democracy. The disagreement is even greater in the case of collective liberalism.

12) *Civility*

Civility is a concern for the common good related to the greater inclusiveness of the collective-self-consciousness of liberal democratic societies.

There has been a widening of civility with diminution of distance between centers and peripheries. Latterly, there has been an attrition of civility with and intensification of demands for "rights," and with less care for "obligations."

13) *Liberal Democracy and Collectivistic Liberalism*

Modern liberal democratic societies have a tendency to turn into collectivistic liberal and populistic societies. The democratic element has led to the expansion of collectivistic liberalism taking its place alongside of constitutional liberalism and narrowing the sphere of individualistic liberalism. The democratic element in liberal democracy inclines toward collectivistic liberalism in which there is a pronounced appreciation of equality. Egalitarianism has two conflicting tendencies within it. One is the denial of particularistic primordial criteria of status and of opportunity; the other is the emphasis on universalistic primordial criteria of status and opportunity. The former would negate descent from particular ancestors as a criterion of entitlement or status and opportunity; the latter would stress membership in the human race or species as a criterion of status and opportunity. Collective liberalism in turn has been congenial to emancipationism and antinomianism.

All of these features of liberal democratic societies have had a considerable influence on the internal structures and external situations of universities.

IV

Interactions Between Universities and Liberal Democratic Societies

University Autonomy and Academic Freedom

University autonomy can never be complete. Universities are parts of the society in which they esist. They have been dependent for practically all of their history on external financial support and this has affected the degree of their autonomy. They have had to concern themselves with the external demand for the services of their graduates and for the requirements of the professions for which their students were to be trained. Governments have frequently in the twentieth century set the conditions for the admission of students to universities and sometimes they have stipulated what should be taught in universities. Private bodies have sometimes exerted similar influence on the placing of a particular subject in the list of subjects taught. Despite these constraints, the universities managed through most of their history to enjoy a very considerable measure of autonomy.

This autonomy became well entrenched in the course of the nineteenth century—earlier in the Netherlands and in the Germanic countries—but it was never complete. In the liberal democratic countries it reached a high point in the first half of the twentieth century, within the limits permitted by the constitutional and political traditions of the various societies. In the first half of that century, central governments by and large abstained from intruding upon the autonomous sphere of universities.

Intrusions have begun to become more substantial since the middle of the 1960s. In nearly every country this has happened. In Germany, the central government which had hitherto always abstained from dealing with universities, except in the interwar period to provide funds for research through the *Notgemeinschaft der deutschen Wissenschaft,* enacted the *Rahmengesetz* which imposes a certain degree of uniformity on university laws of all the state governments. Similar actions have occurred in other countries as the universities and their research have become more costly. In the United States, an executive order of the federal government has intruded very influentially into decisions regarding academic appointments. Most American universities have been compliant with the ambitious demands of the central government and have most recently gone beyond what has been governmentally required in the suspension of the application of intellectual criteria in academic appointment.

It is not that the central governments have taken actions against the resistance of universities to these trends of centralization. On the whole academics have been rather supine in the face of these intrusions into what has previously been regarded as the legitimate autonomy of universities.

A great deal of the impetus to the movement toward greater centralization of governmental authority over British and American universities has come from academics and particularly from economists, political scientists and sociologists. This does not mean that academics have not been jealous about the academic freedom, and especially about their civil academic freedom. On the contrary, much of that civil academic freedom has been exercised on behalf of policies of centralization.

The Separation of Church, State and Society: Consequences for Academic Freedom.

The universities were originally indebted for their autonomy to ecclesiastical powers who wished to protect the universities from their rivals, earthly princes and municipal authorities. That autonomy was not, however, an autonomy *vis-à-vis* the Church. That latter autonomy from the church was usually enjoyed at the cost of the earthly prince. Autonomy from municipal authorities in matters of student discipline, charges for housing accommodations, etc., was widely enjoyed by universities.

Nevertheless, the ideal of a more far-reaching autonomy came into existence. In the oligarchical states of Germany, a *modus vivendi* between the states and the universities was found which, except for a small qualification regarding chairs of theology, excluded the churches from any direct or constitutional influence on universities. In France, the progress of autonomy was unsteady but the coming of the Third Republic conferred autonomy *vis-à-vis* the church on the universities when they finally appeared. In England, after 1870, the church ceased to play any direct part in the affairs of universities, although, in the ancient universities, the Church of England was always a visible presence without any formally assured powers.

DEMOCRACY AND THE MODERN UNIVERSITY

In the United States, which alone of the major liberal democratic countries had practically from the very beginning a constitutional separation of church and state, ecclesiastical bodies continued to exercise influence in colleges of their own foundation until well into the twentieth century.

Yet with all the differences in constitutional provisions and in the role of churches on the highest governing bodies of universities, the modern university has come to enjoy an almost complete autonomy with respect to religious bodies. This is true even in universities which are still legally governed by ecclesiastical authorities.

The invaluable gift of the autonomous university, which the societies of modern times and then the liberal-democratic societies of the nineteenth and twentieth centuries were endowed by the Middle Ages, needed revision or supplementation. It needed revision not in order to bring it into harmony with modern ideas of liberalism and democracy. It needed this revision in order to improve it and to bring to a higher degree of realization the idea which is inherent in the autonomous university. The needed revision was the granting of freedom of investigation and teaching of individuals to go along with university autonomy. It is not that teachers in medieval universities were servile executants in their teaching of ecclesiastically or officially prescribed syllabuses and patterns of thought; teachers frequently strayed from the path of orthodoxy. That is why some universities were forbidden to teach theology and why that subject was confined to particular universities which it was thought easier to control. Nevertheless, the preoccupation of powerful intelligences with ordered knowledge could not but lead to new interpretations of traditional ideas and therewith to discoveries. What was needed was the assurance to these powerful intelligences that their lives and careers would not be damaged by infringements. Nonetheless, academic freedom gradually became installed as the mark of a proper university. It has continued to be so up to the present.

THE BALANCE OF FREEDOM

On the whole, with regard to genuine academic freedom, i.e., the freedom to do intellectual work, the record of governments and churches in the twentieth century and especially since the Second World War in liberal democratic societies has been almost impeccable. The record with respect to the civil freedom of academics is nearly as good; indeed abuse of that part of academic freedom by academics has become more of a problem than infringements by university administrators and external powers on academic freedom in the strict sense.

Market Economy and Private Property

It is clear that universities have prospered from the market economy. The market economy has made the wealth of which universities, whether governmentally or privately supported, have been the beneficiaries. The universities could never have done the many things they have accomplished in research and teaching and in the participation of academics in public life if the economies of their respective societies had not been so productive. Nor could universities have accomplished so much if private businessmen had not given large monetary gifts to universities and created philanthropic foundations which have also made such large gifts to universities. They have also benefitted from the willingness of businessmen to pay taxes assessed at high rates from which universities could be supported by governments. There have been times of economic depression in which the universities were placed in different straits when the economy went into a phase of decline. This affected both state and private universities because the munificence of state diminishes when their revenues fall. Universities which have depended on direct gifts from private beneficiaries have been similarly affected by the state of the market.

The other side of the relationship between universities and the market economy is rather different. Academic economists have not been as generous to the market economy as the market economy has been toward the universities. Economics—theory and research—was more sympathetic to the market economy before it became such a widespread academic subject. It did not choose to be so once it was given a place in the teaching program of universities. Nevertheless it also became more critical of the imperfections of the market and more insistent on the desirability of some governmental intervention to hold in check the injurious effects of the market on those who had failed in it. The humanitarian opinions and activities of academics have helped to darken the reputation of the market economy and have encouraged efforts to supplant it entirely or to restrict its freedom. Some academics in the United States and Germany denounced the market as an immoral institution. But at the same time, other academics did not yield to such arguments. The economists of a few major academic institutions contended strongly for the market even when its reputation in academic circles and in government was at its lowest. Over the past forty years, they have been vindicated. Still, it is very common among academic economists to denounce the market economy and its academic proponents although in very recent years, these denunciations have become less vehement.

Rule of Law

The training of lawyers was from the very beginning of universities one of the major tasks of universities and the teaching of law to future lawyers has remained an unceasing activity of the universities. (Great Britain, and to a smaller extent the United States, were long exceptions to this generalization but they have become much less so in the course of the present century.) In Germany the rule of law and especially the doctrine of the rule of law was to a large extent the brainchild of university professors of law. Yet it must be recognized that the "free school of law"—*die freie Rechtsschule*—which was very critical of the rule of law, was also to a large extent a professorial creation.

THE BALANCE OF FREEDOM

The same is true of the United States. University schools of law have both argued for the rule of law and opposed it on behalf of "sociological jurisprudence." In recent years in the Untied States, the law schools of major universities have espoused the "critical theory of law" which is a successor to "sociological jurisprudence" which by emphasis on judicial discretion has undermined the rule of law and thus endangered liberal democracy. This extension of the powers of the judiciary has had repercussions in the life of universities.

The universities benefitted from living under a regime of the rule of law which has restrained the power and ambitions of civil servants and, in the United States, of state legislators as well. They have benefitted also from the self-restraint of the judiciary in dealing with universities. Until quite recently, judges have usually abstained from exercising jurisdiction over universities, out of respect for university autonomy. This has ceased to be the case.

Academics and students have become more litigious in recent decades, the courts have accepted jurisdiction more frequently. Their record with respect to academic autonomy is mixed.

Academic self-government does not necessary mean collective self-government. It can be oligarchical or even autocratic. There have been autocrats who ruled their universities very firmly and sometimes with very valuable results. The American universities of the nineteenth century were probably those which came closest to autocracy. European universities seldom were autocratically governed. In Germany and Austria, the faculty senate and the senate of the university were made up of all professors—*Ordinarii* or full professors—who exercised much authority in their own jurisdiction. The head of university—the rector, usually lacked in authority, partly because he remained in office for such a short time and partly because the professorial senates were so insistent on their powers.

140

DEMOCRACY AND THE MODERN UNIVERSITY

In France, the professors were voiceless; there was no university, no university self-government and hence no participation by teachers in the government of the "university." The British universities were perhaps closer to representative university government and the colleges of Oxford and Cambridge went beyond that with all fellows being members of the governing body of the college.

The modern British universities began to develop representative bodies when readers, senior lecturers, lecturers and assistant lecturers elected some of the colleagues of equal rank to represent them alongside the professors in the senate.

The changes which have occurred in university government are among the few changes in universities which have moved in unison with the general trend of political life of the past two centuries. There has been a considerable extension of participation in university government. The new university laws which came into force on the continent in the 1960s and 1970s have reduced almost to extinction the professorial oligarchy. The lower professorial ranks and the assistants are not included in governing bodies; nor are students and members secretarial and auxiliary staffs.

American universities came late upon the scene of internal representative government. The powers of these representative bodies, when they did come into existence, were at best consultative. They had little or no legislative power, either positive or negative. Representative bodies of the teaching staff are now widespread in universities throughout liberal democratic societies.

In the United States, junior members of the teaching staffs exercise as much authority as the senior staff; the chairmen of departments have become the equivalents of executive or administrative secretaries of the departments. Presidents have abdicated to a large extent from their previously autocratic powers; indeed, in many cases, they do little more than conform the proposals for decision that have come from below. In very many cases, an academic vice-president or provost deals with the academic side of the university and there, too, departmental government, which is collective and not government by the chairman of the department, has become stronger informally than the president or the provost. Of course, financial decisions have still to be settled centrally.

The tendency has been throughout toward a devolution of authority in the universities. Nevertheless, as in the larger society, as the periphery has become more demanding and as its desires are more heeded, so the central authority is called upon to carry heavier burdens of decision in matters of the collection of revenue and allocations of the provision of innumerable services. For the performance of these activities, a larger bureaucracy has been assembled on a scale unprecedented in the history of universities, whereas universities in the past were conducted with only a very small number of persons who made a career of university administration. This is no longer the case and the consequences are as they are in the larger society: the middle rank of the bureaucracy by small increments, increases in its powers.

Representative Institutions

The participation of academics in governmental representative institutions goes very far back in Great Britain. There the ancient universities were represented by seats which were reserved for them in the House of Commons and filled through elections by an electorate consisting of masters of arts of the universities. The appearance of the modern universities was met by the provision of a seat for London University and a seat for all the other universities combined. No such arrangements have existed in other countries.

As representative institutions grew with the spread of liberalism, university teachers began to stand for election to national legislatures. I think that this began earlier in Germany and in Italy than in other countries. Nevertheless, in the present century there have been many academics who, either on leave or having resigned their academic posts, stood for election to the national legislatures and were sometimes elected. If they persisted in a parliamentary career, they usually discontinued the intellectual side of their academic careers, although they sometimes nominally retained their appointments.

By and large, academics have approved of parliamentary government. At a time when many of them were liberals, representative institutions had a place among their articles of faith. Conservatives, too, accepted them. In the 1920s, with the triumph of the Bolsheviks in Russia and the rise of fascism, the criticism of popularly elected parliamentary bodies became more widespread. Academics, however, were not usually among their more vehement critics. Even in the United States where academic intellectuals stood apart from "party"—and "machine"—politics, more than they did in most other countries, they were not severe critics of the national legislatures and they were not especially active in seeking to reform them. (Woodrow Wilson was an outstanding exception). The interest of academics in the United States was much more attracted to the reform of the Civil service. (It would be worthwhile to know, what part academics played in the institution of the populistic schemes of initiative, referendum and recall which flourished around the turn of the century.)

Even when academics became most hostile to liberal democratic societies, as they did from the 1930s, they did not especially single out parliamentary bodies as objects of their hostility. There were a few severe critics of parliamentary government; some of them supported the granting of increased powers to the executives; some wished to supplement them by a system of corporate representation, second chambers of "experts," etc., but there were few who argued that they should be abolished. Those who took a more or less Marxist view regarded them as part of the "executive committee of the bourgeoisie" and they intimated that the Soviet system of representation would be better.

Nevertheless, during the administration of President Franklin Roosevelt, when many important reforms were enacted by the Congress, academics, especially in the social sciences, followed them avidly and accepted their legitimacy. Still, not many American academics sought elected office. The numbers of those who have done so increased since the Second World War. The reason for their reluctance to seek electoral office in the United States has been that selection as a candidate has generally involved an apprenticeship in local or state politics. This was not welcome to any but a few. The opportunity to exercise power seemed more attractive when it was offered in the form of an appointment to a high position in the executive branch. This was very true in the time of Franklin Roosevelt when American academics, for the first time in the history of the country, entered government in relatively large numbers. (There had been such an entry during the First World War but it was on a much smaller scale and for a shorter time.)

Here and there, academics of some eminence have risen to high office in liberal democracies: Woodrow Wilson, Thomas Masaryk, H. A. L. Fisher, Amintore Fanfani and Luigi Einaudi, Raymond Barre, Ludwig Erhard, Hugh Gaitskill, Harold Wilson were also university teachers. On the whole, the electoral process has not attracted university teachers. Partly it is too arduous and too distracting from the academic mode of life. University teachers are much more inclined toward serving as advisors, as members of specially appointed commissions, and in national emergencies as civil servants. The latter were quite numerous during the Second World War.

Intellectually they have tended to disparage the professional politician. The popularity among academic social scientists of the idea of the "bureaucratization" of society, is an expression of a denial of the value of representative institutions. The fact that so many leading and less leading academics in France and Great Britain before the Second World War and in most liberal democratic societies after the Second World War admired the Soviet Union so passionately is evidence that many of them did not really think that representative institutions were all that valuable.

Freedom of Expression of Beliefs

Much of the progress of genuine academic freedom and of the civil freedom of academics is owed to the increased acknowledgement by the educated public of the dignity of learning, of learned institutions and of the profession of learning. Although academic freedom is not the same as civil or political liberty, it has also greatly benefitted from the expansion and consolidation of the latter in liberal democratic societies.

Freedom of expression in teaching, research and publication was needed if the university teachers were to achieve what they wished and what was expected of them. This is what the unevenly emergent liberalism provided. It did not have an easy birth. It was probably the universities of the Netherlands, the Universities of Leyden and Utrecht, which led the way. Most other countries lagged behind, some very far. The French universities of the *ancien* regime were among the most retrograde in Europe in this respect. The Revolution, which appeared to break the *ancien* regime, did not improve the situation. The age of Napoleon was scarcely an improvement and the successive regimes which followed were little better. The German universities exhibited a closer approximation to academic freedom in practice in the eighteenth century. Perhaps even more important for the establishment of academic freedom was the promulgation of the ideal by von Humboldt and some other German thinkers. By the end of the nineteenth century, the extent of freedom of research and teaching and publication had become a standard for the assessment of universities throughout the Western world. It has become so well accepted in liberal democratic societies but this acceptance has been accompanied in the universities by an unthinking expectation of academic freedom—extending so far as even to cover abuses of that freedom.

Ordered Knowledge

The ideal liberal democratic society is to a large extent a cognitive ideal. It is an ideal of the acquisition of knowledge by deliberate and orderly methods and the integration of that knowledge into theoretical form. This alone has given to universities a position which is a guarantee of their standing and a source of many of their present problems.

The esteem in which universities have been held in liberal democratic societies has been strengthened by the belief that the universities, as centers of scientific research, have contributed and will continue to contribute to the practical benefits of scientific—and latterly, scholarly—discoveries. In the early nineteenth century, before universities had become sources of practically beneficial and economically profitable knowledge, they were being esteemed as parts of the spiritual sphere in which the churches were beginning to renounce their claim to monopoly or at least preponderance.

The liberal ideal accepted, indeed it stressed, the indispensability of rational reflection drawing upon the most reliable information or scientific knowledge for the making of private and public decisions. The market was regarded as the best mechanism to making available the knowledge needed for making private decisions about exchanges of goods and services. The market requires a wide dispersion of that knowledge. It was thought by university economists that a better knowledge of economics would show the advantages of the market for the generation and distribution of that knowledge.

The liberal ideal also proposed or required a wide dispersion of the knowledge needed for public decisions. The original intention of many academic social scientists was to make available the results of social science studies to the widest possible public. It was the expectation that on the basis of such knowledge produced by academics and transmitted to the public, individuals could adapt themselves, i.e., they could control their own actions in ways which would enable each to realize his or her individual objectives and to enable those participating in collective actions, especially those in which authority is exercised, to do so in ways which would be optimally beneficial to all concerned. The same would be true of actions which deal with persons who are not capable of independent judgment, e.g., in schools educating children.

The growth of scientific knowledge has not however been thought to be incompatible with the liberal ideal of the equal distribution of knowledge to the adult public. The liberal ideal of a rationally and mutually adjusting collective life is not so readily adaptable in the affairs of large societies with a high degree of concentration of authority and a fairly high degree of specialization of institutions and of occupational specialization within institutions. Still this is one of the arguments for the teaching of social sciences to undergraduates and even to secondary school pupils.

The idea of representative institutions is an essential ideal of liberal democracy; the pattern of the distribution of knowledge entailed in representative institutions was a concession to inequality. It was in that respect also a departure from the ideal of complete *Mündiokeit.* The development of modern scientific technological knowledge has placed a strain on the liberal-democratic ideal because it renders inevitable a varying, but always high concentration and specialization of knowledge.

The problems created for liberal democracy by the growth of knowledge and its contribution have not been resolved. They create severe tasks both for the center and the parts in which this knowledge is concentrated and by the peripheries which the ideal, and, for a time, the reality of liberal democracy have brought closer to each other.

This anomaly is a ramified consequence of liberal democracy. It was liberal democratic society which has given such a free scope of action to the universities and it is the universities which have generated so much scientific and scientific-technological knowledge. The universities have been to a great extent the beneficiaries of liberal democracy; they grew up and flourished at various times under other social and political regimes but they have flourished especially under the regime of liberal democracy. By their very efflorescence and their fidelity to the task laid upon them by the multiplication of knowledge, they have created a situation which might become a troublesome embarrassment to liberal democracy as well as to themselves.

Rewards Commensurate with Achievement

The idea of the value of individual achievement is almost inherent in universities although there have been times—for example in Oxford in the eighteenth century—when individual intellectual achievement was only one value among others and not usually the main one. In the nineteenth century however, this changed. It was not merely the assimilation of the ethic of individual achievement from the surrounding individualistic liberal society. The change came about from within the universities when increasing emphasis was laid upon intellectual achievement through research. In the course of that century, when prizes were awarded, when honors were conferred and when appointments were made, they were made for the intellectual achievement of individuals. In Oxford and Cambridge colleges, "open fellowship" began to make an appearance; the "closed fellowships" reserved for graduates of particular public schools did not disappear but they ceased to be the only ones.

In consequence of the spread of the ethic of achievement, universities became purified. Idlers and spellbinding place-holders became relatively more rare as the capacity and actualization of individual academic achievement became more widely regarded as the proper criteria for admission, appointment and promotion. The application in matters of appointment of the criterion of past and prospective academic intellectual achievement has always been appreciated in universities but it has not always been applied in practice. For a long time, religious affiliation and affirmation were either explicitly or implicitly treated as being among the criteria of academic appointment, admission to university, sitting for examinations and proceeding to degrees. These have gradually been abandoned in universities in liberal democratic countries. Intermittently, political criteria have been applied in academic appointments at the cost of academic intellectual criteria.

In the United States, where for a very long time, Negroes were never considered for academic appointment, the governmental program of affirmative action and a perverse egalitarianism has reversed the earlier situation. The politicization of universities by their own teaching staffs and the agitation by small circles of students have weakened the adherence to the criterion of academic intellectual achievement in the making of academic appointments.

The humanitarian interest of university teachers at the beginning of the nineteenth and the beginning of the twentieth centuries brought the universities more into the public arena than had been the case in earlier periods when the universities, always concerned to maintain their autonomy, had found a niche relatively isolated from the noise and controversy of the marketplace and the political platform. New developments in the moral life of political democracies have eroded that niche.

One of the changes has been a direct consequence of changes in the interpretation of democracy. The humanitarianism of academics was not engendered from within the universities but the initiative for the entry of academics into the humanitarian movement of modern liberal democratic societies came from within the universities themselves, from teachers of the social sciences and philosophy. The most recent developments, although welcomed and fostered by those parts of the academic profession, has originated outside the universities. The instigation has been a consequence and expression of the general reduction of the distance between the centers of liberal democratic societies and their peripheries.

From the early twentieth century, critics of the universities, especially critics of radical progressivistic inclinations, had censured the universities for their failure to find places in their student bodies for the offspring of the working classes and from the poorer sectors of their societies, more generally.

This criticism was not entirely accurate. Not all university teachers and administrators were content with the high concentration of opportunities for higher education in offspring of the middle and upper classes. University extension classes in the United Kingdom dated from the 1870s. Evening classes at many universities had a similar intention. Birkbeck College, which is part of the University of London had always held its classes in the evening so that employed persons could attend and work for degrees. (It originated in a "mechanics institute"; the very name indicates its intention of providing higher education for manual workers.) Riskin College Oxford, was created with the intention of offering opportunities to workingmen to acquire higher education.

When William Rainey Harper founded the University of Chicago in 1891, it was part of his plan to offer through the extension department higher educational opportunities to those persons who were not well off enough financially to attend the university on a full-time basis.

Numerous statistical studies had demonstrated in the decades before the First World War that the students of universities came mostly from the middle and upper middle classes and more specifically from the families of members of the learned professions—the clergy, medicine and law, business enterprises and higher civil servants, and in the United States from the families of more prosperous farmers. Further investigations of the social origins of university students in Germany, France, Great Britain and the United States between the two world wars, confirmed this "inequality of life-chances." There was little change shown from the earlier studies. Neither university administrators nor university teachers worried much about these facts.

After the Second World War, governments and publicists and particularly the expanded breed of higher educational publicists, began to take these matters to heart. Everywhere the numbers of university students increased, first through support for demobilized members of the armed forces, then through determined efforts by governments to further the admission into universities of candidates, who without financial support from outside their families, could not otherwise attend universities. As a result after the first surge of students who had been kept from university studies by their service in the armed forces, there was a further and almost uninterrupted surge. This was made up to a large extent from students who benefitted from grants by governments and in the United States by the universities from their own resources.

In the United States, with its large Negro population, the demand for the increase in the percentage of students from "minorities," has been very insistent. It is not so pronounced in other liberal democracies but it is likely to increase in those societies, given the increase in the major countries of the numbers of "foreign workers" who are mostly Asians and Africans.

The admission of such students represents more than a mere increase in the absolute size of student bodies which has brought with it severe problems in the supply of qualified teachers, the provision of physical facilities, refectories, hostels, etc. The introduction of many students from cultures alien in their traditions of language, religious belief, and outlook in life, and often of secondary education inferior to that of earlier generations of students, has made the situation more difficult. It has been asserted that the criteria for admission have been unnecessarily exigent. In many cases, it is alleged that the standards of admission are biased against the "minorities."

A similar demand for the appointment of university teachers from the "minorities" has occurred. This had been associated with a readiness to suspend or qualify the application of strictly academic or intellectual criteria in academic appointments.

Those changes in the composition of the student bodies and the academic teaching staffs have brought with them demands for changes in courses of study and syllabuses. New subjects, "Black studies" and "women's studies" have been introduced. There has also been a demand to change the content of teaching away from emphasis on Western civilization and to give more attention to the "contributions" or work of Asian and African authors and female writers who it is argued—quite wrongly—have not been sufficiently appreciated in teaching.

Humanitarianism

A separate tradition, the tradition of humanitarianism had nothing to do with universities in their early centuries. The improvement of the conditions of life of the society and especially of the lower classes was not thought to be anything of interest to universities. It might have been to some extent the coming of political economy under a variety of names into universities which happened first in the German and Italian universities in the seventeenth and eighteenth centuries and then in the Scottish universities in the eighteenth century which marked a turn of attention of some academics to the wealth of societies and their populations and to the physical conditions of the people. ("Political arithmetic" had a transient connection with Brasenose College, Oxford, through William Petty who was a fellow there while serving as professor of anatomy in the University but there is no evidence that he taught political arithmetic while at Oxford.)

It was really in the nineteenth century that persons holding academic appointments began seriously to consider the wealth of nations and incidentally the condition of the poor. I have already referred to the *Verein fur Sozialpolitik* in Germany from the 1890s. The establishment of the Johns Hopkins University in 1875, the University of Chicago in 1892 and the London School of Economics in 1895, greatly enlarged the institutional provision for enquiries into the conditions of the poor. (Previously in those countries, such enquiries had been conducted by private individuals and private charitable societies.) This new field of academic work was often associated with the emergence of a divergent current of liberalism, namely, collectivistic liberalism which turned away from the main liberal tradition which included the free control and disposition of property as an essential feature of the competitive market and of the regime of liberty. There was nothing inconsistent in this change since universities, not being the creations of liberal democratic societies, have had a very variegated relationship with the liberal democratic tradition.

From that point onward, the sociology and social administrative departments of universities, where they existed—some universities were very reluctant to create them—became more intimately related to activities outside the universities to improve the conditions of the poor, the orphans, widowed and deserted women, prostitutes, alcoholics, immigrant laborers, and the whole panoply of activities and conditions called "vice" and "poverty." The turn towards humanitarian concerns among academics entailed not only the introduction of new subjects into universities including the establishment of "schools" within the universities for the teaching of "social work" or "social administration." (This happened especially in some universities in Great Britain and the United States.) The surge of humanitarianism in academic circles was accompanied by actions of academics on behalf of "social reforms" intended to arouse public opinion and to impel governments into measures to alleviate poverty and to control "vice."

From this point onward, university teachers appeared in large numbers in activities performed outside the universities. Hitherto academics had sometimes served on royal commissions of enquiry appointed by governments but they seldom engaged in public agitation. These external activities raised questions about the propriety of such activities and sometimes, particularly in the United States, precipitated some small crises of civil academic freedom. It also brought with it an increased participation of academics in governmental activities which enquired into or which attempted to "solve" social problems.

Somewhat later than the time that academics began to participate in public efforts to disclose by research and to improve by agitation and consultation the condition of the poor and the outcasts of their respective societies, governments began to turn towards academics for advice and for special services. The First World War which burdened the established civil services led to the invitation or assignment of university teachers to special administrative roles. This was especially true in the United States which has a less professional civil service than the other more or less liberal democratic countries. These activities receded once that war was over but never to the level of the prewar period. The great depression of the 1930s and the Second World War brought many more academics into governmental service as administrators and as advisors. It also increased their interest in extra-academic matters.

Efficiency, Productivity and Rationalization

The momentous achievements of scientific military technology in the Second World War and thereafter and the upsurge of belief in the pervasive indispensability of scientific knowledge threw up many more bridges between the universities and the world outside them.

Between the two world wars, there has been some worry about the adequacy of representative institutions and the other institutions of liberal democracies to survive and to deal adequately with the problems of contemporary liberal democratic societies. The firm grip of the Russian Communists on the empire which they inherited, the abolition of liberal democracy in Italy by the Fascists in Italy and the tribulations of liberal democracy in Germany and its overthrow by the Nazis against the background of the apparently insuperable economic depression shook confidence in the effectiveness of liberal democratic institutions.

In response to these doubts, there were proposals to make government more scientific or to give more powers and responsibilities to scientists in governmental affairs. These ideas were very valuable and the fact that some of their proponents were communists or sympathizers of communism reduced their persuasiveness. Nevertheless, the experiences of the war, and the continuing series of great scientific discoveries brought scientists—mostly academic—into a more active role in the public life.

Correspondingly, governments began to spend much larger sums of money on scientific research and scientific education. The beneficiaries of these increased expenditures were the universities which appreciated greatly the benefits and thought little about the costs.

When governmental expenditures on science and universities were relatively small, there was little public attention directed toward them. The prestige of scientific knowledge and of the universities, which were so intimately associated with its growth, was very high and the expenditures were neither begrudged nor closely scrutinized. This seemed to be a very happy moment in the relations between universities and liberal democratic societies. It was only an interlude of largesse between a period of scarcity and one of scrutiny and continued largesse.

The largesse was not very much appreciated in the universities because no largesse could ever be generous enough to meet the much expanded demands of scientists and universities for financial support on a scale which was never sufficient to meet the ever expanding demands. The scrutiny entailed some sort of intervention into the work of academic scientists and this was not in accordance with the traditional freedom of academic scientists to choose their problems and to do their work without having to worry about governmental scrutiny and direction.

One of the subjects opened up for scientific investigation by economists was the study of industrial productivity. Much ingenuity and work went into these studies. After the Second World War, governments became concerned about the productivity of their industries. International industrial competition had been discussed by economists ever since Great Britain began to be displaced by Germany and the United States as the leading industrial power. The study of such matters in universities and by research institutions staffed by university economics departments made progress. The impact of these intellectual developments was twofold. Universities came increasingly to be expected to contribute to improved industrial productivity by their scientific research. Another consequence was that universities began to be questioned about their productivity. This question had never been asked of universities before. The universities were now being asked whether their teaching was efficient; the same question was asked about their research. It was asked whether pure or fundamental research was efficient and whether it was economically productive. No satisfactory answers were given to these questions. Perhaps none can ever be given in view of the nature of the product. Nevertheless, the questions continue to be asked. The closer relations between industrial firms and universities and the increased concern of governments about whether the money they spent on research in universities is being efficiently and productively used have put greater pressure on the universities than they had ever experienced before.

The reversal of the traditions of university autonomy and scientific freedom has probably not been very far reaching. It has certainly not been as far-reaching as it could be. Academic scientists have retained a great deal of their traditional freedom but they also lost some of it. The fact is that the relationship between universities and the governments of liberal democratic societies has become much more differentiated, more intimate and intricate as well as much denser than it had ever been before. It has also become more troubled, more beset by doubts.

Concurrently, new scientific discoveries and their application in scientific technology in private industry and commerce have also become much more intimately connected with each other. Scientific discoveries in certain fields have turned out to be much more immediately and more specifically applicable than had been the case with scientific discoveries up to the beginning of the Second World War. This has made industrial and commercial entrepreneurs more eager to profit by the application of scientific knowledge and to encourage such research by the provision of financial incentives. Thus academic scientists have been drawn into connections with private business enterprises more closely than they had ever been. They have been attracted by the prospect of more support for their research which was becoming ever more costly and also in many cases by the prospect of private enrichment.

These new relationships and questions have been embarrassingly experienced for other reasons as well. The demand for funds for research is insatiable; at the same time, universities have become more costly to administer as they have grown in size and in the scale of their teaching and research activities. University teachers and administrators are in search of funds in ways which they have never been before. Universities have never before been expected to pay their own way, except for institutions of marginal intellectual importance which have supported themselves mainly from the tuition and other fees paid by students. Nowadays, at least in Great Britain and the United States, they are being pressed to engage in money-earning activities to meet their increased costs—as well as to contribute to the economic growth of their societies. These situations have added to the difficulties of conducting autonomous universities with internal academic freedom along traditional lines.

Disparagement of Tradition

Scientific research in the universities like science everywhere and at all times have been focused on original discovery. From the "Scientific Revolution" of the seventeenth century many scientists and the handful of scientific publicists of whom Francis Bacon was the greatest have regarded the traditions of ancient Greek and medieval science which they inherited as something to be transcended and discarded. Although great and eminent scientists like Werner Heisenberg and Michael Polanyi and a famous philosopher like Karl Popper have laid great emphasis on the importance of traditions on scientific discovery, most scientists have had little respect for tradition. Social scientists in the universities have shared that view. They have thought that tradition lives in simple, primordial societies but it was thought by them to have no place in modern progressive societies.

The only places left for the appreciation of tradition in universities were the humanistic faculties which studied the great works and societies of the past. In the past fifty years the humanistic disciplines have experienced a marked change. They have come to regard the works of the present and recent past to be as worthy of the attentions as the works of the remoter past. Classics as an academic subject has declined in prominence. Historical studies have had to make way for the study of recent and even contemporary history.

The influence flowing from the humanitarian sensitivity of university teachers has taken a further turn against tradition in the humanities. There "the tradition" has come into heavy weather.

The demand to give a larger place to cultural creations of the "minorities" in university studies overlaps with a more comprehensive hostility towards the tradition of the great works —called disparagingly—"the canon" of Western civilization. The school of literary criticism which has recently gained the ascendancy in the humanistic faculties of universities of the liberal democracies is very hostile toward the traditions of liberal democracies and toward traditions in general. They are opposed to any sort of authority except that of the heroes of contemporary literary criticism such as Paul de Man and Jacques Derrida and above all to the philosopher and historian, Michel Foucault. They are hostile to intellectual traditions, even to knowledge itself which, because it has been received from the past, is regarded as "oppressive." In extreme statements, they say that even language is "oppressive" because it provides established forms for expression.

This antinomian body of beliefs is prominent mainly in the humanistic disciplines and particularly in the study of modern literatures. It has, however, made inroads into the social sciences, and even into the classical and oriental parts of the humanistic disciplines. In the social sciences—not in economics—the work of "deconstruction," i.e., of devaluation, takes the form of "unmasking" and "demythologization." It draws something from Marxism and although it is generally free from affiliation with any existing parties there is some sympathy with the "green" or "alternative parties." Its political sympathies are sometimes populistic and anarchistic. It is in any case, irreconcilably hostile to liberal democratic society.

At present, it is in the ascendancy in certain branches of academic study. There are counter-tendencies and traditional modes of scholarship still strong in many of these fields but the practitioners of those modes are timorous and on the defensive. Although these practitioners of the traditional modes of study do not wholeheartedly support the antinomian views, they are reluctant or fearful of opposing them. Only a small minority speak out against them and they are pilloried as dogmatic reactionaries.

The humanistic faculties which were once reservoirs of indifference to politics and of a politically conservative outlook have now become very politicized. Indeed they are the most politicized parts of the universities.

Thus within the universities in which they hold remunerative appointments and in which they exercise their authority over students, they oppose the traditions without which universities could not exist.

V
The Contributions of the Universities to Liberal Democratic Societies

The universities have contributed to their liberal democratic societies certain services which have helped those societies to function and they have strengthened the attachment to certain values or beliefs which are constitutive of liberal democracy.

On the most practical side, they have trained physicians, scientific research workers in medicine, biology, agriculture and the physical sciences. They have trained all sorts of engineers who, taking over the task from engineers trained by apprenticeship and periods of study in very specialized institutions, have continued together with chemists the elaboration of the technological apparatus of the modern economy and contributed to its productivity. They have trained medical research workers who have made it possible to control many diseases and together with the agricultural research workers who have increased agricultural productivity, they have lengthened the life span of human beings in many countries and not just in the liberal democracies. They have trained persons who have administered modern governments and business enterprises more or less efficiently and honestly. They have not only performed research and applied the results of research, they have also offered expert advice to governments and large organizations and perhaps helped them by their advice to function more efficiently and thereby maintained the morale and confidence necessary for the effective functioning of liberal democracy.

VI

What Universities have not done for Liberal Democratic Societies

Baseless Accusations: Religious Beliefs: What have universities failed to do? They have above all failed to replace a lost religious faith in many human beings' lives—becoming more troubled intermittently—by their inability to hold confidently a view of the world which gives meaning to cosmic and human existence. That, however, is a task the universities never undertook. As long as the churches were able to do what it was in their province to do, the universities worked alongside them in a division of labor which left the final truths of existence to the churches while they attempted to understand and explain according to the methods of valid and reliable knowledge. When the churches declined in credibility, the universities, except those, as Max Weber called them, "grown-up children," who thought that scientific methods could supply answers to all the questions which serious enquiring minds could ever ask, continued to perform with increasing success those tasks which were appropriate to them.

Baseless Accusations: Indifference of Society: There are certain charges against the universities of which I wish to dispose. The most general of these is that they are "ivory towers." This accusation has been made for a long time. It was wrong when it was first made. Three of the four faculties of the universities if the Middle Ages were concentrated on the training of young men for the learned professions the services of which were demanded by society. The accusation has always been false but it has been especially false in the past few centuries. (It might be better if the universities were more like ivory towers than they are today.)

Another charge is that they do not serve society's "needs." Quite apart from the problematic term "needs" which is usually some desire of the critic purporting to speak on behalf of the sections of the population whom the critic has not consulted and which has not delegated him to speak on its behalf, the charge must be rejected out of hand. Large parts of the university are devoted to working on topics which are of practical social interest in technological and engineering studies, in medicine, in physics and chemistry, even astronomy and astrophysics—subjects once thought impractical except for the applications in navigation, all of the social studies except for history. Philosophers even seek to show their relevance to practical life. Logicians are indispensable to the information sciences. So it goes. The universities have been accused of being insensitive to environmental problems; all the environmentalist arguments are drawn from scientific knowledge.

Baseless Accusations: Moral Indifference of Scientists: Two other closely related charges are that the academic scientists are uninterested in the problems raised by their discoveries, and that they are incapable of giving answers to them.

The first charge is not usually directed against universities as a whole but against scientists mostly in universities. It says that scientists take no responsibility in themselves for the practical repercussion of their discoveries. This accusation is wrong in two respects. One is that many scientists have indeed concerned themselves with the ramifications in society of their discoveries. The entire movement for the control of nuclear weapons began inside the Manhattan project; Leo Szilard, James Franck, and Harold Urey initiated the discussions. The "movement of the atomic scientists" as it was called was a product of the initiative and courage of some of these scientists. There was a wave of naive but genuine civility at the end of the Second World War among scientists who had been engaged in the work which was directed toward the invention and construction of nuclear weapons. (It did not last; it fell into the groove of collectivistic liberal partisanship and helped to make internal discussions about nuclear weapons more vehement and less civil.) Nevertheless, for what has been accomplished the scientists of the Manhattan project belie the charge made against them. On this point alone, in connection with which the charge was first made, the charge is simply wrong. It is wrong also on the assumption that the remoter practical consequences of scientific discoveries can be foreseen by anyone. Furthermore, scientists alone are not responsible for the practical applications of their work. Practical applications are decided on by politicians and by civil servants, by businessmen, managers and engineers and workers. Nowadays if something goes wrong at a nuclear power station or in a chemical plant, the accusations are immediately leveled against businessmen and managers. Workers are invariably not drawn into the target of accusation although in a number of cases, it was negligence on the part of a worker which precipitated the accident. In any case, it is not sensible to think that the scientists who made a discovery would be in a position to watch over all of its proper uses. Scientists do not rule society, their critics do not wish them to do so and even if they have greater powers over economic life and over technology they would not have the knowledge to do what their critics suggest they should do.

The critics of scientists and of the universities to which the criticisms are extended are naive in their belief that scientists could solve the problems to which their discoveries give use. There is a hidden, unthinking, unintended compliment to the moral wisdom of scientists when it is suggested that they can foresee all the main applications of their discoveries and can resolve all the moral problems to which the applications of their discoveries give rise.

Genuine Problems: Wisdom and the State of the Humanities: A society without wisdom is bound to go astray, and a liberal - democratic society is no less liable to do this than any other type of society—perhaps more so, as university graduates who have not received some of the intellectual preconditions for wisdom come to constitute an increasingly large fraction of the adult population. This is where the humanities are failing to serve the good of a liberal-democratic society.

163

THE BALANCE OF FREEDOM

The study of the great works which are the subject-matter of the humanities may foster the growth of wisdom in those who study them. Wisdom cannot be taught and the students are too young and too inexperienced to give birth to it. It can be elicited only by those who had a mind for it, and that can be achieved only in the years of maturity and the study of great works—the "canon" now disparaged by teachers. But that is not the way in which teaching is done nowadays by many teachers of the humanities.

Humanistic studies moved from the task of finding and living in accordance with the right pattern of life, through the study of the great intellectual works of antiquity into the painstaking emendation of texts and later to the pedantic study, in great detail, of unimportant authors and events, and most recently, into an extraordinarily frivolity and neglect. The transformation came about gradually and unwittingly. At first, the secondary task of humanistic scholarship was the discovery and collation of surviving manuscripts with the aim of making the texts as pure as possible, that is, as close as possible to the state of the text when it left its author's hand. This was a work of tremendous importance. It was a task which challenged great intelligences and called forth impressive qualities of memory and imagination.

With the increasing sensitivity to contemporaneous truths, the study of modern languages and literatures came into the programs of academic humanistic studies, the emendation, purification and emitting of texts aiming to establish what an author had really said and the preparation of learned editions of great works reclined. The invention of the printed book had rendered much of that important activity of emending and editing texts superfluous. There were not many modern authors as great as Plato and Aristotle or Horace and Virgil worthy of such work, and the study of the contemporary recently living great authors offered little in the way of an exemplary pattern of life in accordance with which a scholar could hope to form and live his own life.

In consequence of this, and with the attendant increase in the number of research students writing dissertations for the doctorate—from quite different causes—innumerable doctoral dissertations were produced and many of them were published. They had to be as detailed as the much richer documentation permitted. The small number of worthy subjects and the great number of persons to work on them, with the obligation to mankind an original contribution to knowledge resulted in a widespread trivialization of subjects. Such "original" research led to the production of a flood of boring books and an inevitable weariness and disinterestedness of much exhausting research. The vision of a way of life faded away nearly completely. That is one of the causes of the crisis of the humanities which has been aggravated by the wantonness of a desperate profession. What is now called "theory" in the humanities is the misguided effort to find new tasks for the humanities.

The movement toward "theory" in the humanistic disciplines has received an influential embodiment in the technique of "reconstruction" which has recently gained the ascendancy. Its derogation of the "canon" is an effort to deny the validity of the tradition which ranks literary works in accordance with intellectual and literary criteria other than individually variable likes and dislikes. It is against the traditional canon. What it is really trying to break is the tradition of Western liberal-democratic society. It is a form of antinomian political radicalism with scraps of Marxism and psychoanalysis, supported in the most far-reaching and subtle form in some of the work of the philosopher and historian, Michael Foucault. It is hostile to intellectual traditions, even to knowledge itself which, because it has been received from the past, is regarded as "oppressive." Even language according to this new movement, is "oppressive" because it provides established forms for expression.

This antinomian body of beliefs is prominent mainly in the humanistic disciplines and particularly in the study of modern literatures. It has, however, made inroads into the social sciences, and even into the classical and oriental parts of the humanistic disciplines. In the social sciences—not in economics—the work of "deconstruction," i.e., of devaluation, takes the form of "unmasking" and "demythologizing."

The current efforts made in the humanistic disciplines to overcome their desiccation by launching themselves into "theory" cannot be accused of narrowness. They are very broad. Their leaders hold forth on all sorts of subjects which they have not studied, economic history, sociology, philosophy, comparative religion, etc., there is no subject which they do not venture into to rediscover their own image of the world. Nor can it be said against them that they are not interested in a way of life. They are interested in a way of life—it is nothing other than complete emancipation from all traditional ways of life. Humanistic "theory" is very political but its politics are those of antinomianism—although probably in any particular situation their views are those of the radical or emancipationist variant of collectivistic liberalism. This is not very fertile ground for the growth of wisdom or for the growth of civility, either within the university or within society. In any case, they find liberal-democratic society utterly abhorrent. It embodies all that they would destroy.

Their political sympathies are generally populistic and anarchistic. In the United States, this hostility to the tradition of liberal-democratic societies has another facet: the accusation against the great literary and philosophical works of Western civilization as "sexist, racist and imperialist."

Traditional modes of scholarship are still strong in many of these fields, but the practitioners of those modes are timorous and on the defensive. Although these practitioners of the traditional modes of study do not wholeheartedly support the antinomian views, they are reluctant or afraid to oppose them. Only a small minority speak out against them and they are pilloried as dogmatic reactionaries.

Thus within the universities in which they hold remunerative appointments and in which they exercise their authority over students, they oppose the traditions without which universities could not exist. Needless to say, they are irreconcilably hostile to liberal-democratic society.

The Failure of Academic Civility: Scientists have indeed also presented liberal-democratic societies with problems which are beyond the capacities of the scientists and their societies to solve in any definitive way which commands far-reaching consensus. The problems generated by the advances in biomedical sciences and biomedical technology are unprecedented. They have raised questions about the control of reproduction, the prolongation of human life, the prolongation of life of particular individuals, and the manipulation of species with which no societies have ever been faced before. Scientists, having contributed their mite to the abandonment of traditional religious beliefs and their associated ethical beliefs now find themselves confronted by problems which they are ill equipped to solve. It is not that the traditional religious beliefs and ethics offer any clear solutions. It is only that the new problems disclose the moral threadbareness of the scientific and technological professions as well as the inadequacy of our traditional religious and ethical beliefs and those naturalistic, secularistic and romantic dogmas which pretend to replace the traditional view.

It is not that there have not been great scientists and physicians who have also been humane and generous persons and who have taken seriously the future of their respective societies and of all mankind.

The once widespread notion that scientific training purged an individual of prejudice and partisanship and that scientists could therefore speak for the common good—and that scientific knowledge itself offered such knowledge of the common good—has turned out to be a generous delusion. I do not intimate by this statement any slur on the character of scientists, many of whom are guided by a disciplined love of truth which is exemplary. But being exemplary is not the same as being typical.

These charges against academic scientists and the universities which educate and nurture them are ridiculous. They are ridiculous because despite their criticisms of scientists and universities, they attribute to scientists powers which scientists do not have and which are not in their capacity as scientists to have. The criticisms which they direct against scientists are made from a scientistic standpoint. The scientistic standpoint asserts that scientific knowledge provides the sole necessary foundation for moral judgments; it asserts that scientific knowledge permits prediction of the future and that scientists also have special political gifts which entitle them to rule in their capacity as scientists. (I cite here the very popular Godkin lectures of the late Charles (Lord) Snow Science and Government in which exactly these arguments are put forth.)

Such views have no intellectual defensible basis. The universities cannot justly be accused of failing to do what cannot be done by anyone. There are probably still some scientists who themselves believe these things. They do not however blame scientists or science for these limitations, they blame politicians and national public for not giving scientists a free enough hand.

Genuine Problems: Specialization: Another criticism of the universities is that their scientists and teachers have become very specialized. There is no doubt that specialization has pernicious consequences for the specialists and for the universities in which they work. Specialization is however inevitable as well as desirable in scientific research. Scientific research has had to become specialized. No scientist can work over the whole range of science or even over his own discipline. A scientist who wishes to discover something which has not been discovered before and to add something of importance to what other scientists know must read or at least look at a vast quantity of published material and nowadays, unpublished material as well. It is true that much of this material is of little consequence and an experienced scientist learns how to dispense with it. Even then a large amount remains. The huge number of practicing scientists in nearly every field and the large number of journals created in order to publish the results of their research means that in order to go beyond what has already been done, it is necessary to work very specifically. It is also necessary to use very accurate equipment which ordinarily requires the use of assistants who in the course of time will produce a very considerable number of papers of their own. The more specialized the scientists, the more dispensed are the colleagues apart from his own immediate collaborators, assistants and students, who can appreciate what he is doing, assess it helpfully and in their turn offer him something which he can use for his own understanding.

Here and there, there are scientists who read widely in the scientific literature and who know things outside the immediate neighborhood of their own research. There are even scientists who read in philosophy, literature and history. They are not dilettantes; they could not be and still continue to be productive and respected scientists. They are however not many and they cannot change the culture and action of their colleagues, even though they are admired for the breadth of their interests and knowledge. They cannot be imitated.

The high degree of specialization has borne great fruit. The achievement of recent science would not be possible without it. The practical benefits as well as the intellectual achievement of scientific research have depended upon it. It is probably impossible for science to make progress without specialization. It is true that some of the great steps forward have been made by scientists who have broken out of the narrow boundaries of a specialized field of research but those advances could not have been made by persons who had not been rigorously trained in a specialized field of research. Furthermore, once a great advance has been made, specialization becomes a common feature of the new field.

THE BALANCE OF FREEDOM

It is perhaps not the specialization of research which is injurious to the university but the narrowing of the collective-self-consciousness of the specialized scientist as a member of the university. These specialized scientists, whose scientific interests and activities are much narrower than the interests of their departments, remain generally very concerned about their departments. Their interests do not generally extend to their university as a whole. It is probably a very exceptional scientist who regards the university as much his own as he regards his department. One could see this in the United States, at the time when the federal government was pressing universities to appoint members of the minorities to their teaching staffs. In Columbia University when the federal government threatened to suspend all grants to that university if it did not conform to the government's demand that more members of "minorities" be appointed to their staffs, the members of the scientific parts of the university wished that the university would yield since the point of contention was an appointment in a humanistic department. The scientists felt that they would not have to modify their criteria of appointment because they were confident that the government would not dare to tamper with the scientific work done there; it was too important. Similar instances can be cited of this disregard for the standard of the university as a whole.

Such indifference to the well-being of the university as a whole is injurious to a university in several respects. One of the most important is the function of the university as the site of a compelling intellectual culture. A university is not just an administrative unity which has a unified budget and which handles the administration of salaries, the construction of buildings and the provision of the numerous services such as maintenance, registration of students records, the award of degrees, etc. It is a collectivity in which outstanding individuals embody and exemplify the intellectual standards and the academic ethic. There are never very many such persons but they play a disproportionately influential role in the maintenance of the standards of a university. If that is lacking, a university becomes slack, its standards and expectations deteriorate. A great university can descend into mediocrity, mediocre universities remain mediocre or become worse.

Specialization is not the sole cause of this academic incivility. It might even protect a small part of the university from the erosion of standards indirectly consequent on this lack of concern for the common good of the university. The intellectual morale of the academic specialist is also maintained much more directly by the standards of the individual's particular department and by the standards of his specialist colleagues in other universities in his own country and in other countries.

VII

The Universities and Civility

This is a very rough but approximate account of the relationships between the universities and the main features of liberal democracy. It is clear that the universities owe a great deal to liberal democracy and that liberal democracy owes a considerable part of its successful functioning to universities.

Liberal democracy needs civility, i.e., a concern for the common tool. What have the universities contributed to this? Before attempting to answer directly this difficult question, it is desirable and reasonable as well to suggest that civility involves detachment from conflicting interests and an imagination capable of envisaging a solution which is more than a compromise between the conflicting interests and which takes into account consequences for third parties. It is a rare quality and it is probably never found unalloyed. It is always contained with partisanship within the mind of each individual who possesses some of it.

Despite their often crude and unashamed espousal of partisanship, civility is probably most often found among politicians with long experiences because it is they who can see the entire society somewhat more frequently (seldom very frequently) than other persons except experienced lawyers who often have a comprehensive perspective over the entire society. What about academics? Can they achieve and exercise some of the civility needed by a liberal democratic society for its maintenance?

Karl Mannheim thought that the *"freischwebende"* intellectuals, the detached intellectuals, free of obligations and devotion to social classes, political parties and other parochial interests and ideals, might be capable of speaking for the common good. He thought that they could do so by amalgamating the partial perspectives of the contending parties into a single wider perspective. This might well enable them to become more objective and more capable of discerning the common good. For this he was almost everywhere ridiculed. (In the recent revival of interest by radical sociologists in his ideas about the sociology of knowledge, this is one aspect of his work which has been allowed to rest in oblivion.)

Yet, Mannheim's idea should not be rejected without further ado. It ought to be seriously examined. Although vague, it is not in itself ridiculous. Scientists and academics achieved the high status which they long enjoyed because it was thought that being disciplined to observe and analyze, despite their own personal predilections and pride, they possessed the objectivity necessary for dispassionate judgments, as true as the evidence allowed.

Governments over the past half century have frequently turned to academic scientists to do research on particular problems. They have also been invited to give advice to politicians and administrators at all the higher levels of authority because there was confidence that the scientists could rise above vanity and partisanship. They were asked to tell what "science" knows in particular problems and to recommend alternative policies and they were even encouraged to recommend the adoption of some particular policy because there was confidence that they would fairly assess arguments for and against any particular policy and that they would bear in mind the interest of the entire society.

172

Their association with universities was thought to be a further guarantee of disinterestedness. The university was believed to be an exigent institution; nothing less than truth was to be expected from it or from those who were members of it.

In serving governments on advisory capacities in this manner, academics conformed with the liberal democratic ideal of infusing sound scientific knowledge into the conduct of practical affairs. They were able to do this because of the good reputation universities had acquired as institutions devoted, in an utterly disinterested manner, to the discovery and enunciation of truth.

The advice given by academic scientists has not always been good advice, in the sense that the results of policies based on their advice did not turn out as had been hoped. Often the advice given by academic scientists, including social scientists, has been disregarded because the persons advised received contradictory advice from other advisers, or because they themselves had opinions of their own which were inconsistent with the advice they received. Nevertheless, the advice of scientists was frequently sought because it was thought that scientists were politically disinterested, desired to serve the common good, and were capable of objectivity in judgement.

Politicians and administrators, i.e., laymen without the discipline and knowledge provided by scientific training and activity, could not themselves assess the validity of the knowledge drawn upon by their scientific advisors. The validity of the results of research gained by scientific methods can really be judged only by other scientists who have mastered the field into which the investigation falls. Scientific studies are often so highly specialized that even an authority in one field of science cannot usually pass judgement on the knowledge gained in another field. Certainly very few laymen can verify the scientific assertions made by a scientist. Even if a layman consults scientists who have divergent views about the same subject, he is scarcely in a position to adjudicate their differences and to decide correctly by himself which one is right. Hence it is important that the scientists be regarded by the laity as trustworthy. This means that the universities must be regarded as trustworthy.

Universities have been respected because they were thought of as dealing with very important subjects and because it was thought that those subjects were dealt with honestly and impersonally, that is, without concern for private pecuniary gain or for fame. That is why in the course of the nineteenth century, liberal democratic societies and those which were less liberal and less democratic fostered the development of universities. They believed that universities, like the church and judiciary, were necessary for society; they attributed a high moral value to them. It was thought that they served the ideal of truthful knowledge. The functions of universities were not just practical; even when they performed such functions, they were esteemed for producing the truthful knowledge which was necessary for practical functions such as the care of health or the practice of law. But the main function seldom if ever adequately articulated was the custodianship, transmission and enlargement of the various bodies of truthful knowledge. Universities were maintained because the centers of their respective societies wanted them, not necessarily for their own practical or spiritual benefit but because they thought that universities were needed for society in the way in which religious institutions, literature and art, justice and internal peace, majesty and ceremony, were needed. A society without these things would be an incomplete society.

Universities moved forward as the churches diminished in their centrality. The universities overlapped in their function with the function of the church which was to link the society with the transcendental realm, i.e., a realm which transcended the material interests of individuals and of the various groups making up society. The universities like the churches before and alongside them represented to their societies an objective value or values beyond the interests or desires of any given group within the society.

The universities and their academic staffs usually did not think in these terms which envisaged the university into an earthly church. But they did accept that the universities should stand above or beyond the practical interests in any class and that they must make the scrupulous methodical pursuit of truth in research and teaching their first obligation.

This was an important function to perform in a liberal democratic society. The liberal component of the market, the aspiration toward individual achievement and the working of the mechanisms of the allocation of rewards commensurate with achievement sometimes produced injurious consequences to be moderated by the idea of the moral order of the whole of society. There is also another potentiality in liberal individualism. This is the emancipation of the individual from all the constraints of rationality and tradition. This is a danger to liberal democracy. Similarly the democratic element in liberal democracy had a tendency toward populism which placed the desires of the populace and of its proponents and their conception of its interests above all else. This, too, is not the only thing in democracy but there is a tendency in that direction which has to be kept in check for the concern of the whole.

VIII
What can the Universities do for Liberal Democracy?

Liberal democracy is an ideal form for societies which are differentiated, in which the various sectors of society, each of which has interests and ideals which are in conflict with the interests and ideals of the other sectors, have an opportunity to realize some part of their interests and ideals. This differentiation is an inevitable consequence of the size and tasks accepted by the society. It is also the ideal form of society for vigorous individuals with ambitions and ideals of their own. Liberal democracy is a regime which acknowledges this differentiation of ideals and interests. Other types of regimes, and particularly totalitarian societies, attempt to suppress them and to bring them under their own central authority those which cannot be suppressed, and to deny the reality of those types of differentiation which they cannot suppress and which they cannot dominate.

Because it is differentiated and calls for differentiation, liberal democracy requires consensus, i.e., a collective self-consciousness embracing most of society. It does not require complete consensus; complete consensus would render liberal democracy largely superfluous. It requires a measure of collective-self consciousness. This collective self-consciousness is sustained by a common language, the strength of a common authority making and applying law over a common, bounded territory. It needs traditions which keep before it an image of a long and common past. It needs emblems of an effective center and sub-centers. It needs institutions and individuals who are emblems of the whole and who can speak and act to bring forward the whole so that it overshadows its parts.

The different sectors of liberal democratic societies must be kept in a peaceful balance or equilibrium with each other. It is not possible for this balance or equilibrium to be achieved or maintained only by rational bargaining with each other and by explicit compromise. Some differences of ideas and interests can be bargained over and fixed by contract but not all can be rendered compatible with each other by this technique.

The concern for the whole is a transcendental value. It is not only transcendent of the material interests of the various sectors of society; it is also transcendent with respect to power and the desire for it, with respect to authority and the desire for it, and with respect to prestige and pride and the desire for them.

Can the universities perform this function nowadays when they are needed more than ever, now that the churches have renounced their aspiration to provide for mankind an objective transcendental ideal which stood for the whole in time and society?

Not everyone in the society needs to be completely civil to the rest of society or to a particular group other than his own at all times. Even if it were desirable, it is neither necessary nor possible. The centers of society must be more civil than the peripheries, although these peripheries too must possess some civility; there must be sub-centers of high degrees of civility scattered throughout the society.

I do not think that the universities, either the greater or the lesser, are representing this civility to their respective societies. They are not very civil inside themselves having become desegregated by earnest specialization and by a self-indulgent antinomianism. The tendencies which make them uncivil internally make them uncivil in their activities and beliefs regarding the public sphere.

Concluding observations

My conclusion from all these observations is that the universities in the liberal democracies will continue to perform important functions in training for those professions which require, for admission and practice, knowledge of the matters which universities can and should properly provide. They will continue to do important research, although as the results of intellectually important as well as practically useful research can nowadays be more speedily converted into practically useful and profitable activities, more of such research will be done outside the universities.

They will continue to nurture and display a relatively small number of persons of exemplary devotion to truth in their respective fields. All of these are functions necessary to the well-being of liberal-democratic societies. They will continue to provide consultants and advisers.

As to the provision of an infusion of civility in liberal-democratic societies, I do not see the universities performing this function. They have become too uncivil internally and also too self-indulgent and lacking in firmness of character to withstand the pressure on universities of external incivility. Administrators of universities are usually too weak in character, they are harassed by costs which exceed revenues and by the ceaseless desire to increase their activities and to stay on the right side of uncivil proponents of external and internal demands. If universities were less before the eyes of the public, it would be better for them and for their liberal societies. But I do not think that this is likely in the near future.

I think that, for the time being, liberal-democratic societies which cannot do without many of the functions which universities perform for them, must make do with a very small contribution from them to the exhibition and diffusion of civility throughout their societies. They will have to do as well as they can with the civility produced by some politicians and lawyers and by the saving remnant of ordinary citizens scattered throughout liberal-democratic societies.

Addendum: On Private Universities

I was originally invited to treat the special situation of private universities in relation to liberal democratic societies. I have found it desirable to change the terms of reference which I was asked to observe. My reason for doing so is that the major private universities, which are to be found only in the United States, seem to me to have renounced the advantages of being private and to have behaved in recent decades little differently from state or governmentally supported universities in the same category of distinction. (There are a handful of private universities in Great Britain and Germany. They are very new and they operate on a small scale and under very hard circumstances. The prevailing academic and political opinion—even liberal democratic opinion which should be sympathetic with the idea of private higher education—is not sympathetic with the notion of a private university.)

Private universities have, in principle, the advantage of a greater autonomy than is enjoyed by state or governmentally supported universities. They can be more free from the influences which flow from political and public opinion. They can go their own way and they can avoid the wrath, often quite irrational, of state legislators. They do not have to divert their attention to maintaining the favor of state legislators and the higher administrators of the state government. They can—again, in principle—introduce novel educational programs. They can introduce new fields of study and their teachers can teach and do research with greater freedom and less apprehension about falling foul of demagogic legislators, unfriendly newspaper editors and publishers, aggrieved citizens, often aggrieved on trivial and poor grounds, but able nonetheless to agitate the political atmosphere and to cause academic damage.

The advantage of a private university lies, other things like intellectual tradition being equal, in the presence of a strong president. State universities or governmentally supported universities even were they are autonomous, are bound by the need to cultivate and persuade state legislators and by the rigidity or imperiousness of ministerial civil servants. The president of a private university is free of these. If he is courageous enough and imaginative enough he can do things which the teaching staff and the board of trustees might be reluctant or unwilling to do; he must be able to carry them alone with him but it is exactly in that capacity that his strength lies. At one time, the presidents of American private universities were often persons of strong character and a serious concern about academic things. I think here of Daniel Coit Gilman at Johns Hopkins University, William Rainey Harper at the University of Chicago, Nicholas Murray Butler at Columbia University, Charles W. Eliot and Lawrence Lowell at Harvard University and others who have left their mark on their respective universities. There have also since the Second World War been exceptional individuals as presidents of private universities such as Wallace Stirling at Leland Stanford University, Edward Levi at the University of Chicago and James

Conant at Harvard. Of course, exceptional persons are always rare. They would not be exceptional if they were not rare. Still, such exceptional persons seem to have become rarer since the Second World War.

The tasks of university presidents have become much more difficult in the past half century. The increased revenues of universities, private and public, are never enough; despite large "development departments," the president has become an indispensable and perhaps the most crucial participant in the raising of funds from private patrons, prosperous graduates, private foundations, and so on. There is much more to administer in universities than there used to be and much larger administrative staffs to deploy and supervise. University presidents in private universities, no less than in state universities, have now to contend with large teaching staffs to whom much authority had devolved, *de facto.* Academics are now more demanding and more fractious than they were when the disfavor of a president was almost a notification of dismissal or a blocked career.

The new type of university president, even if an imperious person, works under great constraints within the university. His intervention on behalf of an appointment of a particular candidate would be regarded very adversely by the members of the department to which the candidate might be appointed. Furthermore, external opinion, and not just governmental action, compels compliancy on the part of a president. In the United States in recent years, the program of affirmative action, i.e., the policy of appointing members of "minorities," meaning mostly Negroes and Puerto Ricans, and women and if possible, American Indians, have sapped the will of presidents. "Affirmative action officers" within the university, usually aggressively accusatory in their language, lay the president open to the charge of "racism" if he does not "aggressively" foster the appointment of blacks, and the charge of sexism, if he is lukewarm about the appointment of women.

DEMOCRACY AND THE MODERN UNIVERSITY

There is much more to be said about the hamstringing and distraction of the presidents of universities in the United States today and all of it would apply almost equally to the presidents of private universities as well as to the presidents of state universities.

A strong president of a private university can however make a difference. I mention, for example, President John Silber of Boston University and President Peter Diamentopolos at Adelphi University in New York. They are both strong and courageous presidents and they both have valuable ideas about how to improve their respective universities but they encounter much hostility and resistance from the teachers who wish not to be aroused form their customary slumbers. When they are aroused, they seek to encompass the dismissal of their presidents.

Private universities, if their endowments and their revenues from gifts, research contracts, etc., are large enough, do not have to allow the size of their student bodies to grow as do the state universities. The six leading private universities in the United States are much smaller than the six leading state universities. This would seem to afford many advantages, e.g., smaller classes, less bureaucracy, higher morale and better relations between students and teachers and between academic staff and administrators. Such differences do in fact exist and undergraduates at one of the major private universities (as well as the leading liberal arts colleges which are almost all private) probably receive better teaching along the lines of a better worked out syllabus than does an average undergraduate at one of the immense state universities. But in the private universities, too, the standard of education is being adulterated by obligatory "minority studies" and by the capitulation of the demand for more appointments according to the criteria proposed by "affirmative action." These occurrences are consequences of the weakness of presidents—equally weak at Stanford and Duke, both private universities—and at Wisconsin which is a state university.

THE BALANCE OF FREEDOM

If the private universities in the United States had stronger presidents, that would still make a difference but they would have to contend with recalcitrant academic staffs who are determined to share in the government of their universities, whose beliefs are reinforced by the knowledge that they are shared by the academic staffs of other universities all over the country.

What this betokens for liberal democracy should be very apparent from my analysis in the body of this essay. Autonomous universities are important participants in pluralistic societies. Their autonomy is decisive for their contribution to liberal democracy. To gain the benefits of autonomy both for the university and for society requires strong leadership, firmly supported by members of the institution. That is lacking today in the United States because of the obstacles maintained by the antinomian outlook of many teachers and the civilly uninterested specialization of many others within the universities. In the face of these powerful forces, the difference between private and state universities is not significant. So much the worse for liberal democracy!

SIX

LIBERAL EDUCATION AS A PREREQUISITE FOR LIBERAL DEMOCRACIES

Walter Rüegg

I
Liberal education as the powdered wig of outdated societies

Herbert Spencer introduced his famous essay on "Education, Intellectual, Moral, and Physical" with an observation made by Alexander von Humboldt: An Indian of Orinoko who does not care about physical comfort, yet will work hard for two weeks in order to produce skin dyes which exalt him in the eyes of others. An Indian woman who would not hesitate to leave her hut completely unclothed would not dare to violate the convention of her tribe by going out of doors unpainted.

By this and similar anecdotes Spencer wanted to show that liberal education is on the same level as the customs of primitive tribes for it deals only with adornments of the mind and not with real values. It does not concern itself with matters which are truly useful and necessary but only with prejudices considered by the society as a *sine qua non* of a good education.

To a utilitarian point of view liberal education appeared and appears also today as a luxury, as the powdered wig of outdated societies. In fact for centuries it enjoyed as a typical form of upper-class education a high prestige among people who worked for practical ends, from factory hands and farmers to industrialists and representatives of big business. In the salons of the bourgeoisie the liberally educated graduate was indeed treated somewhat condescendingly, but with a certain respect. Liberal education opened the hearts of the daughters of the rich and the bank accounts of their otherwise so matter-of-fact fathers. The sons of the most robust self-made men were anxious to conceal the naked figures of their fortunes in the mantle of the socially indispensable liberal education.

With the democratization of modern societies the social glamour of liberal education disappeared. In the eyes of Spencer liberal education consisted mainly in the ability to quote Latin phrases, to allude to Greek mythology. These times have gone. Some old-fashioned scholars like myself may still take offence at a mispronunciation of a Greek or Latin word. But I cannot remember to have heard in the last few years somebody pronounce a Greek or a Latin word outside classical or medieval scholarship. Recently I tried to allude in a scholarly work to the Nephelococcugya where Socrates is shown by Aristophanes sitting over the clouds. But I had to drop this allusion, because I was warned that neither the Nephelococcugya nor even Aristophanes' clouds are any more known by an academic public. In the British parliament it would be unthinkable that the Prime Minister could, as in Pitt's time, quote Virgil to be answered by the leader of the opposition with a corresponding quotation from Virgil while everybody in parliament would enjoy this literary parrying. The best known names of the Bible and of literary works are Hecuba to the majority of society. The representatives of culture rank socially far below the big names of sport and mass media. The road to success not only financially but also socially leads no longer through liberal education but through a special training of mental or physical faculties.

It may be argued that liberal education has always been the prerogative of a small sector of the society and that uneducated people have always been more interested in sensational rather than in cultural values. As a matter of fact the *artes liberales* were the education for the *liberi*, the free citizen. All others were excluded from political and cultural participation. In modern democracy the situation is quite different. Through membership in parties, trade unions and similar pressure groups or through special abilities each adult person, regardless of his social origin and his education, has access to political and cultural opportunities. To a large extent these opportunities include symbolic forms, values, works, and institutions created in the past by elites formed by liberal education. The modern public, even if its major part lacks liberal education, shows an astonishing interest in these creations. From the *"Zeit der Staufer"* in Stuttgart 1977 to the "Age of Chivalry" in London 1988 innumerable visitors queued up before scores of exhibitions which showed the treasures and accomplishments of the past. Millions look to television series on historical and cultural themes. Novels and even scholarly works on historical topics became bestsellers.

Already in 1946 Karl Jaspers stated in a paper on "The European Spirit" that in relation to the global order and to the two new world powers, the European tradition would develop into the life of a museum in which we would be tourist guides to the world: "To be this...would still be a calling. We must not depreciate what is left to us in such a life: a world of memory, precious for all men. To live as an interpreter of a world of memory precious to all men, who lovingly attend to what must never be lost would not be to live badly."

Since 1945 Europe has regained its economic, scientific and also some political dynamics. But regarding its culture the only dynamics consist in an unparalleled expansion of museums and in the transformation of churches, castles and whole villages into museums. This interest in the past is quite understandable. The more modern and unstable a society is, the more it looks for symbols of security in its past. But what is the role of liberal education in this romantic search for a tradition which in real life seems to be outdated?

In this chapter I would like to develop the following thesis: Liberal education has its origin in the social demand of new economic elites for literary transmitted historical models of political and social behavior which were lacking in their primordial traditions. In modern democracies the need of such symbolic models is even stronger, and if it is not covered by liberal education it degenerates into a romantic or dogmatic understanding and abuse of the past. Therefore liberal education is a prerequisite for liberal democracies.

II
The Origin of Liberal Education

Liberal education appears in Western civilization when number and word, the two fundamental symbolic forms of social interaction and social institutionalization, dissociate themselves largely from their magic and mythical ties and become rational tools for the direct satisfaction of needs and for the mastery of individual and collective life. Professional groups, merchants, bankers, lawyers, administrators, contractors, and managers specialize in the development and administration of the new social means of communication, that of money and the written word. They form new ruling classes besides, and often in conflict with the old aristocracy. This social change which occurred from the eighth to the fifth century B.C. in Greece, in the first centuries B.C. in Rome, and in the European cities from the thirteenth to the sixteenth centuries A.D. presents three fundamental difficulties which increased in modern liberal democracies.

1) Since number and word, as means for bartering goods and ideas, have detached themselves from their sacral and

feudal ties, they act as explosive forces and destroy the traditional worldview and social order. Social mobility, differentiation, and disunity of society result in the fact that one and the same person continuously has to learn new social roles whose demands may contradict each other. The personality of the individual and a corresponding humane order in a given society depend on the degree to which different roles may be combined in a structure that is strong enough to stabilize tensions between them, but at the same time is open enough to allow the liberal development of man and his society.

2) In traditional societies the individual is connected to its origins through symbolic interactions that have a magical or mythical character and link the mundane to the transcendental order, without any distinct time dimension. Man in a mundane order comprehends himself as part of the divine nature or salvation and thus justifies the relevant social and political structures. Rulers find their legitimacy in their identification with, or at least in their symbolic connection with, the divine powers. The ruler is perceived as God, as the son of Heaven, as God's representative or scourge. Only if the descent of the actual mundane order from a timeless transcendental order is questioned will the past appear as a reality alien to the present. The reassuring continuity of tradition is lost, and legitimization has to be found in stories and history, in which the estranged past makes sense to the present.

3) In the ruling families of traditional societies, political attitudes, rules, values, and role patterns were passed on by oral communication. They were embodied in living family members and their friends as well as in previous generations. Through direct interaction with political men, the politician-to-be not only acquired the necessary knowledge but was also introduced into the role patterns, values, and attitudes that would enable him to make the right judgments and decisions and thereby gain power of persuasion. The advantage of such primordial forms of socialization, the comprehensive and

strongly emotional transfer of different role patterns, with all its nuances, imponderables, even contradictions would provide fertile ground for political education in the orientation toward personal models related to the individual.

New political elites cannot legitimize themselves through old family traditions and ultimately through connection with the transcendental order. They have no ancestors whose stories and history could serve as positive or negative role patterns for their social and political behavior and actions. Compared with the old elites, who explain their leading roles by their nature (*physis*) they must acquire political skills through a formalized learning (*techne*). In the Athenian democracy of the fifth century B.C. the sophists professed to give young men a completely higher education as a preparation for public life. They were so successful that not only the new elites but also the old aristocracy paid high fees for such a civic education of their sons.

That was the beginning of the liberal education, the education of the free men in a more democratic society. It added to the physical and military training intellectual studies dealing with numbers and words which later were called the trivium of the three verbal arts, grammar, rhetoric, dialectic or logic and the quadrivium of the four mathematical arts, arithmetic, geometry, music, astronomy. The essential part of the political training consisted in rhetoric which cultivates language as the symbolic form of moral evaluation and political action. It aimed, on the one hand, at the right use of words according to the task, the audience and the moral consequences of the verbal act and it developed into a very elaborated art of composing speeches, letters and other literary forms. On the other hand, it implied the study of literature in which men of the past had written down their concepts, experiences and evaluations of human actions. Since they describe also how important decisions under uncertainty were carried out and what kind of moral, political, and social problems were involved they had for the new elites the same manifest function as the case studies in modern schools of political sciences or business administration; but their latent function was the search for a symbolic legitimation through the interaction with models of the common cultural past.

Whereas the Greek founding fathers of liberal education accepted as models only persons and documents of their own past and treated foreign languages as barbarous, in Rome and Renaissance Europe symbolic forms of alien though historically related cultures served as models for the higher education of their elites. This enlargement found its expression in the notion and the meaning of the *studia humanitatis*. Through his interaction with written documents of alien *humanitas* the student had to form his own *humanitas* which combined encyclopedic knowledge and mastery of language with moral responsibility. The term *studia humanitatis* was coined and its concept developed by a *homo novus*, a social and political newcomer, Cicero, in the first century B.C. The *studia humanitatis* were revived in the fourteenth century primarily by social newcomers and were also successful with the offspring of the old nobility which had lost the formative power of family tradition in the economic, social, and intellectual crises of their societies. The *studia humanitatis* gave a new direction to the liberal education all over Europe as the expressions "humanities" in English, *humanites* in French, *lettere humane* in Italian, *die Humanioren* in German indicate.

As I mentioned, for Cicero the historical models were not confined to the Roman tradition. He was the first to announce publicly that the statesman had to listen also to the voices of a people which the Roman public used to despise as *graeculi* and whom he praised as the *genus humanissimum*. By accepting the literary forms of this politically disdained foreign nation as suitable models for civic training the deep-rooted human conflict between in-groups and out-groups was dealt with in a way which had far-reaching consequences for the history of mankind: thanks to the liberal education, enriched by the Roman concept of the *studia humanitatis* people learned eventually to understand aliens as being equal or even superior in their symbolic expressions without the bond of a common creed in the transcendental order.

III
The Development of Liberal Education in Early Modern Europe

Liberal education based on the Roman concept of the humanities was introduced in the European Renaissance also as a program of civic training for new elites, who, through the use of written symbols, could aspire to political power but lacked the necessary primordial traditions. But there were two important additional features which increased the dynamics of liberal education in modern Europe: 1) the institutionalization of secular religiosity by the dialogical structure of communication; and 2) the perception of man as an animal symbolicum. These features stem from the Judeo-Christian concept of God, who, by his will, created the world and entrusted it to the free will of man and, throughout history, continued, and strengthened by the sacrifice of his son, the alliance with his creation.

1) In antiquity, the divine and the mundane order were closely interwoven. Thus liberal education, as a training for the highest mundane activities, came into conflict with the transcendental order only when Christian religion transformed ancient civilization. The liberal arts, based mainly on pagan literature, had to be justified as creations of God. They were compared with flowers that have their roots in the wide meadow of the Holy Scripture; their power was to be found in these roots and not in the fading (pagan) leaves. By this and similar metaphors—e.g., as honey that may be collected from all kinds of flowers and blossoms, or as pagan spoils brought into the temple—liberal education as part of the mundane order could be legitimized by the authority of the transcendental one. This symbolic authority had its institutional counterpart in the monopoly exercised by the clergy over liberal education. From the 11th century on it was challenged by the

new urban classes who needed the three Rs and also the liberal arts for practical purposes. But this use of written symbols was deprived of transcendental legitimization and was often contrary to the norms professed by the church, as illustrated by the conflict between the growing importance of money economy and the condemnation of usury by the church. The main religious problem for the new elites was to reconcile their mundane activities with the transcendental order.

Scholasticism pursued the liberal arts as a part of the *vita contemplativa* which aimed at elucidating the ultimate truth in the symbolic constructions of the transcendental order. When they became part of everyday life, the *vita activa* had to be legitimated as an autonomous social dimension of mutual human interactions. The Renaissance humanists tried it in theological terms by ranking the patriarchs of the Old Testament with their family and social life higher than the martyrs and monks. Philosophically they emphasized the free will, diversity, and social responsibility of the individual against the intellectual universals. Above all they encouraged the direct meeting of laymen with God's word by a dialogue between man's personal experience and the transcendental order. San Bernardino of Sienna illustrated this new religious approach in a sermon he gave in 1425 exhorting his audience as follows: "Would it not give you great joy to hear and see Jesus Christ, Saint Paul, Saint Augustine, Saint Gregory, Saint Hieronymus and Saint Ambrosius and the other saint masters? Then go and read your books as often as you like; speak to them and they will speak to you. They will hear you and you will hear them."

The dialogical structure of communication with the transcendental order had its counterpart in the historical dimension. The Romans, in studying the writings of the Greeks were more interested in the timeless lessons to be drawn from them than in the specific situations that the authors had to cope with. They had no difficulty in reconciling their own religion with the Greek mythology. The humanists of the Renaissance were aware of the fundamental differences between Christian and pagan cultures, but also between their own time, the Middle Ages and Antiquity. By focussing on the language as personal and interpersonal expressions of purposes, experiences, judgments, and creeds, past personalities, epochs, books, and other symbolic forms could be perceived in their own perspective. Liberal education promoted the search for historical authenticity in restoring and interpreting sacred and secular texts, in discovering historical forgeries like the "donation of Constantine," and in the critical reconstruction of past lives, institutions, societies and epochs.

2) Liberal education meant the application of the rules and practices of the several liberal arts leading to philosophical thinking and moral education. In antiquity the ideal politician was seen as a combination of an orator and a philosopher. The second feature of Renaissance added to the Roman concept of liberal education was an understanding of language which included poetic imagination. This conception considers man not only as an animal rationale, but rather as an animal symbolicum, who seeks to give meaning to his hopes and fears, illusions and disillusions by the symbolic forms of his cultural life.

The change in the perception of language occurred when in the 14th century Petrarca experienced in the writings of an ancient author a combination of emotional and rational expression in all its richness but also in its individuality and, when his new approach to language found enthusiastic approval and emulation amongst his contemporaries. The so-called rebirth of antiquity was perceived by them as a revival of the muses. In consequence poetry was considered as an important contribution to the education of the new elites. The perfect statesman should not only combine the qualities of an orator and a philosopher but also those of a poet. By this qualification he would have access to the world of symbolic expressions that also take into account the irrational and emotive pattern of human interaction. Thus, poetry became the broadest category of human knowledge. The laurel wreath of the poet, the *laurea*, was regarded as the highest intellectual honor and was bound up with the right to teach in an university.

"Le style c'est l'homme même" this phrase coined by the scientist Buffon in the 18th Century illustrates the importance the symbolic signification of language had achieved in the formation of European elites. It is also a suitable motto for the microsociological aspect of liberal education. In his famous essay on written communication, Georg Simmel denoted "distinction" and "ambiguity" as the two most important sociological categories of human communication. Whereas oral communication can supplement the distinction and ambiguity of language by modulation, gesture and other bodily expressions, writing operates through the objectification of the subjective. If man is conceived as a being identical with his writing, then orthography, grammar, rhetoric, poetic and literary criticism gain a pedagogical, even a political, dimension. The proper choice and use of words becomes a political weapon as it can be seen at the present time, but which was already felt at the end of the 14th century by the ruler of Milan who complained about the letters written by the humanistic Florentine chancellor that they did him more harm than an army of a thousand cavalrymen. Liberal education also leads to proper reading which allows one to discover, through the written word, both the open and the hidden characteristics and purposes of other people, other social groups, other value orders, other cultures. It is a necessary precondition for meaningful social and political action in a pluralistic world in which written symbols play a fundamental role.

At the beginning and in the course of the early modern age which eventually developed in liberal democracy, the humanities and the liberal education were successful because they helped societies, in which new economic forces challenged traditional structures and values, to transfer and to adapt the old values to new structures. It is true that the very same principle which was instrumental for this success contributed also to the shortcomings and aberrations of liberal education. Taking language as the essential human activity implied several dangers. Focusing on symbolic forms by which man tries to grasp rationally and emotionally the secrets of the mundane and the transcendental order, liberal education steered a narrow philosophical course between the Scylla of nominalism which regards language as a purely subjective invention and the Charybdis of realism which considers it as the manifestation of an objective reality.

Searching in literary works for models of proper writing and moral behavior implied the temptation to imitate slavishly a specific style or to copy alien customs, values and religious beliefs. This aberration was already refuted in the first *querelles des anciens et modernes* which took place between 1400 and 1600. Leading humanists made quite plain that it was not the model as such which had to be imitated but the attitude and disposition embodied in it. Since the most prominent model, Cicero, had stated that every word has its meaning in the community in which it is placed, the moderns must express themselves differently to the ancients and can even become superior to them. So Dante and Petrarch ranked higher than Virgil or Homer. But as the later *Querelles* show, this attitude toward the classics did not prevail. In the schools the prose of Cicero and the verse of Horace and Virgil were aped. The cultural advantage of a literary canon which was common to the European elite was overshadowed by the monopoly which enjoyed—at least in school—the classics of antiquity.

But the most important shortcomings resulted from the very anthropological limitation of considering language as the essential human activity. Its merit was the promotion of a new civility based on symbolic forms of verbal and especially of literary communication. Liberal education had become a prerequisite for the old aristocracy as well as for the new urban elites and enabled them, despite the political divisions into national states and despite the many religious and political conflicts, to develop a homogeneous European society which displayed dynamic forces unequaled in the history of the world. This creation of a European society can basically be explained by the common liberal education of the ruling elites. A Polish, English, French or Swedish politician did not have precisely the same concept of Christ, Cicero or Aristotle. But in their education they had all been exposed to the same great personalities of the past. Fed by the same symbolic food, they had developed homogeneous symbolic forms that allowed social communication despite political and religious rifts. Humanistic diplomacy and the great peace conferences between 1648 and 1815 are held in greater respect today than they were before Versailles and Trianon. The scientific and literary efforts of the sixteenth and seventeenth century are no longer discarded as polyhistory, polymathy or prolixity. We have learned how deeply we are indebted to them.

But, on the one hand, the prominence of literary education developed into a formalism of social behavior which was experienced as a tyranny and provoked the outcry of the *retour à la nature*. On the other hand, it did not take into account the fundamental importance of another human activity, that of manual labor, its social actors and the social change they provoked by the industrial revolution.

IV
Liberal Education in Modern Democratic Societies

This brings us back to Spencer's criticism of liberal education and to the romantic interest which contemporary societies manifest for their past. My rather excessive historical analysis of the origin and development of liberal education permits to draw some conclusions for its place in modern liberal democracies:

1) As we have seen, liberal education was introduced for persons in urban occupations where written language has become an important basis for coping with existence; from a

sociological point of view, they belong to the so-called third sector which performs services by the production, administration and distribution of information. Liberal education was simultaneously the consequence and the vehicle of social and political emancipation of professional groups trained in the use of written symbols. Contemporary societies are more and more composed of professional groups who work with numbers and words in research, business, finance, administration, industry, communication, education, transports of persons, goods and information. Therefore our so-called postindustrial societies need liberal education even to a greater extent than preindustrial societies. Writing on computers makes things even more abstract than doing it by pen or pencil; it objectifies and estranges the concrete environment. It was and still is the task of liberal education to promote the proper writing, i.e. to use words and numbers not only as means for practical purposes, but also for the composition of symbolic pictures that will make sense in an estranged world.

2) Liberal education enriched by the humanities laid the foundation for a liberal world view by which human behavior and action are less judged by determined value orders than by the power of their meaningful discourse. In the dialogical structure of communication, concepts and values do not confront one another by argumentational strings of abstract logic, but by individuals expressing their own situational definitions. A liberal world view not only endeavors to evaluate the abstract truth embodied in different points of view, but tries to see them as symbolic structures of conflicting actors in relation to their situation and to one's own and tries to find solutions for a common order which respect mutually the free expression of such symbolic construction.

3) Liberal education means the translation of alien human forms into one's own. This is particularly true of translations from foreign languages. One of the Romans' most important contributions to liberal education was the conversion of Greek works into Latin. But also in one's own language the task of

liberal education is to translate a linguistically formed code of meaning expressed by others with its inherent values into one's own. Through translation the stranger becomes not a brother but a partner and possibly a friend.

4) Liberal education as a way of social and political training consists of learning how to understand alien people as personalities with their own complexity of feelings, endeavors, thoughts, experiences, and actions through their own testimony. This in turn contributes to a better self-understanding. From Cicero on, people who had received a liberal education frequently stated that they found in books not only friends with whom they could always talk and receive answers for their problems, but also models that guided their political actions and helped them gather self-assurance and strength.

5) The humanities replaced missing or distanced family traditions of political and social experiences with the study of literary testimonies of personalities who stamped history with their works and thus not only offer case studies of social and political action but also contributed to the material and mental foundations of the present. To become involved with such personalities means to have an improved understanding of the prerequisites and possibilities of one's own political and social actions in a liberal sense, i.e., in openness toward alien humanity. This holds true also, and even particularly for modern democracies in which all adults are supposed to act as responsible citizens.

6) Classics are authors in the forefront of humanity. They open the way to new insights, cast light upon uncertainties, inform about obstacles and opportunities, encourage those who march behind them and demonstrate how one can find his own way of life. Europeans encountered such classics in their cultural past, in the pagan and Christian literature of antiquity. The elites were eager to understand them in the original and to translate them for themselves by reading but also for a larger public by publishing translations, from Greek into Latin, from Latin into the vernacular. Soon they included

into the classics the great books of their own national and of other European traditions. Today the variety of classics may present difficulties in establishing reading lists for schools and colleges. But it should be seen not as an obstacle to but as an enrichment of liberal education, provided that the study of literature allows the readers to enter into a dialogue with important personalities, to confront his own views with theirs, to perceive himself from their position and to assert his standpoint against that of aliens by means of language which is also one of the fundamentals of political liberalism.

8) Liberal education is not the product of a stable political and social order. Rather, it can be seen as the attempt to find new symbols of security in an out-of-joint world in which the primordial and transcendental orders are challenged by the rationalism and materialism of an urban society. This applies to the modern urbanized world even more than to old societies in which the cities were relatively small centers in the vast rural periphery.

9) Liberal education is based on man's definition as a being able to cope with language. In contrast to the *homo faber*, the Greek sophists already attributed to the *homo loquens* the capacity to establish social and political values and institutions. The modern notion of man as an *animal symbolicum* binds the language to the world of poetry, of myth and religion and enables liberal education to learn how to use language not only as an instrument for material goals but also for the benefit of the common cause in liberal democracies.

SEVEN

SCIENTIFIC MAN: CURSE OR BLESSING FOR LIBERAL DEMOCRACY?

H. Maier-Leibnitz

Evidently, being a physicist, I am biased because I do not feel that my colleagues and my students and I myself are a curse to society. I came to physics from mathematics and from astronomy where there are so many interesting things to learn and to see and to understand and try. I started doing research in atomic physics but I had an opportunity to move to nuclear physics which at the time was no more important for applications than astronomy was, but it held great hopes for fundamental discoveries. After the war, our activities shifted toward what is now called nuclear solid state physics, investigating the structure and dynamics of crystals and other materials, mostly using gamma rays and slow neutrons from the new research reactors. This finds many applications of a scientific nature in physics, chemistry, and biology, and one of our students was lucky in getting a Nobel prize for his doctoral work, discovering the Mössbauer effect which still leads to about a thousand publications a year the world over.[1]

A scientist is motivated by the wish to learn and understand, and to help keep the treasure of knowledge and add to it by his research and by passing it on to the next generation in a form which allows them, too, to help create the future, the future of knowledge and its consequences. All this gave us no reason to doubt that becoming a scientist and increasing the knowledge is legitimate.

The discovery of nuclear fission was a surprise to everybody including the discoverer. Nobody could foresee that such a remote and purely scientific field like nuclear physics would lead to a terrible application like the atomic bomb which really raises the question: Is all science a curse?

Our own relation with applications was not spectacular. I became a professor of technical physics. The founder of our laboratory was Karl von Linde who has done much to develop modern refrigeration. My predecessor had made fundamental contributions to superconductivity. We tried to teach physics with an eye on possible applications in many fields, and we had contacts with industrialists who asked our advice. The year 1955 was the first Geneva Conference on the Peaceful Uses of Atomic Energy, and from then on we had contacts not only with industrialists but with politicians.

The situation as it existed then is a good starting point for our subject. Adenauer, like other statesmen in the world, saw a chance to promote research in Germany which had fallen behind in long years of isolation, and at the same time to gain access to a new technology which held great promise to furnish cheap energy and which could be considered to be a symbol of the beneficial influence of science and technology on economic growth and on progress in a wider, not precisely defined sense. The industrialists were eager to fill the gap in technological knowledge and in international competitiveness which was a consequence of the war, and they hoped that the scientists with their international connections could help them to bridge this gap. The scientists were willing to contribute what they knew, and of course they set their hopes on increased promotion of research in general.

As for the application to nuclear energy, there were two tendencies. One, supported by the politicians and some scientists, mainly from the school of Heisenberg but others, too, pleaded for the creation of nuclear research centers where they would have a leading role in the development. Others, and I was one of them, thought that industry should take over what at the time was beginning to be called Research and Development (R&D), as soon as possible. The research centers were founded and still exist, but after a time their activities developed away from reactor technology to more general tasks, and industry took over its own responsibilities.

The transfer of knowledge from research to industry is a process which has influenced technological progress, not in the beginning of the industrial revolution, but for more than two hundred years now, mostly without interference from the governments. In the beginning of the new rapid development after the Second World War, men like Karl Winnacker, the head of Hoechst Chemie, who was a sort of master of the industrialists, had insisted that industrial responsibility must mean that industry should not accept financial aid (and the ensuing influence) from governments, but this sound proposal did not last.

As for science at universities, the consequences of this development were helpful: Research there increased in full freedom. The activities of the professors in nuclear energy were limited to membership in committees and some occasional consulting; and as time went on, there developed some fruitful cooperation with their colleagues at the research centers where of necessity a certain fraction of the research had to be of a basic nature.

If we look back today at the situation then, are there reasons for reproaching the scientists? I should say mostly no, if we do not object to their doing research at all. They accepted an offer to promote their research. This is legitimate if they had reasons to believe that this could be in the interest of mankind. "Knowing is better than not knowing": this is what all scientists and scholars believe. Is nuclear energy an exception? I do not know of anybody who at the time would have believed that, even if some scientists like Fermi and James B. Conant were not sure that nuclear energy was really useful.[2] We could have thought of two questions. The first is: Was nuclear energy needed in the world, then or later? And the second: Is nuclear energy safe, or are there dangers for people or for nature? It is strange that the first question was rarely asked at the time, probably because everybody thought that nuclear energy would be much cheaper than fossil energies. This turned out to be an error, in part because oil became cheap soon afterwards, and the first cost estimates for the new technique were too low. Anyhow, today nuclear energy has an economic advantage in many countries, so the objection is not important. However, nuclear energy was not really needed at the time, and even now there are enough alternatives, at least if one does not believe in the danger of fossil fuel consumption for the environment. The great energy need will come not now but in fifty years.

As for the dangers of nuclear energy, maybe we did not speak enough of them at the time, but we were sure and we were right in assuming that they could be mastered. I shall not repeat here the arguments which I think are convincing even if the public discussion is extremely confused. As a whole, I feel that it is correct to say that nuclear energy is not a reason to declare that science is a curse to mankind.

Is there something else for which the scientists can be reproached? They did more than accept freedom for research: they told what they knew to those who wanted nuclear energy. Knowledge must be public property if it is to be used at all, and there can be no court to decide which information should be withheld so long as those who receive it are not criminals. It is true that in public discussions today, politicians and industrialists are often attacked as if they were criminals but this just shows that the level of such discussions is deplorable.

All this leads us nowhere. If we want to decide whether science is a curse, we must not seek scientists who may be guilty. We must ask whether the world would be better off with science or without it. We must question the saying: knowing is better than not knowing, in a general way.

The greatest stumbling block for a belief in science as a blessing is, as everybody knows, the atomic bomb. We scientists, and especially we nuclear scientists, are forever worried that our research has made possible such a frightening development. But the question is: are we responsible? C.F.v.Weizsäcker has said that we feel responsible for it like a father feels responsible for bad deeds of his children. But is responsibility the right word for this?

The fundamental problem with the results of all basic research is that they are not predictable because they are new and nobody could have foreseen them except by doing research himself. Nuclear physics, before the war, was a field which was as far from applications as astronomy. We all knew that in a single nuclear transformation, a million times more energy appears than in the burning of an atom of coal. But we also knew that ten thousand times more energy was needed to produce such a transformation, and nobody had thought of a way to circumvent this. After the neutron was discovered, one knew that every neutron could produce a nuclear transformation with gain of energy, but again, to produce a neutron one had to try ten thousand times. Therefore, no serious person could ever have warned of the dangers of nuclear energy before the new and totally unexpected phenomenon of the fission of uranium was found.

The meaning of this can only be: all research that leads into the domain of the unknown may be helpful, or it may be dangerous. If we want to prevent damage at all costs, all we can do is prevent research generally, prevent scientists (and probably all scholars) from doing research. But this would mean: knowing is worse than not knowing, and we now must look for arguments that might support this new thesis.

Is knowing worse than not knowing? The question must seem absurd to a person who believes in the power of reasoning. Can knowing be dangerous? This sounds different. New knowledge allows new thinking, new decisions, new actions. But knowledge is always imperfect, thinking is imperfect. New decisions may have consequences which have not been foreseen, or they may lead to actions by others whose behavior is unpredictable. There are many courses by which new knowledge may lead to serious errors, and this has been the subject of endless discussions in the past. Since I am a physicist I do not know enough to analyze them. However, today, when the increase of knowledge has become so fast, we are all daily confronted with examples of practical problems. Rational and irrational reasoning is involved, values are brought into play, and the influence on public opinion has become a battlefield in the fight for ideological and political power.

Being not a philosopher but a physicist, I shall keep away from the fundamental discussions and instead stick to what I have seen and done and learned myself. I can think back some seventy years, and the first thing I want to say is that I cannot believe that anybody would wish that science should not have lead to many of the changes which since have made our lives more safe, more comfortable, and potentially more rich. We live much longer, we lose less time and well being by pain and illness, we spend less time and effort to make our living, we have nearly unlimited access to learning and culture; the standard of living for the average citizen and for the disadvantaged is much higher than it was ever before. Much of this, of course not all, has been made possible through progress in science and technology, enough indeed to make the idea to abolish science sound absurd.

If this is true, then the problem cannot be how to avoid knowledge but how to avoid its misuse. And this is a problem where the scientists and engineers are no more the main actors. They can give ideas about what can be done to avoid damage, and warnings. Indeed, all the important environment issues have been attacked first by them, often many years before the environmentalists made them their target. In 1959, for instance, there was an intensive study on water pollution in Lake Constance, leading to demands for reform which were followed only decades later. Personally, I have been somewhat connected with the problems of nuclear energy, in committees and as vice-chairman of the reactor safety commission. Later, I wrote a book together with an adversary of nuclear energy, Peter Kafka, who fears the dangers he thinks it presents to mankind. However, his motivation goes farther. He believes that everything should be done to slow down the technical progress which by its speed prevents the normal adaptation, which should be by trial and error, to new developments. And he believes in the advantages of a simple life.

This now is an attractive idea. I have recently had the opportunity to visit the places where I lived as a child, and I found that most houses and things were still there. But everything was crowded with new buildings and development, and the greatest factor, and really the symbol of the new time, was the street traffic by its noise, smell and its gigantic dimensions, which go far beyond reasonable demands on freedom, comfort, and necessity.

Let me try to analyze this problem a little farther. I remember seeing endless rows of cars on American highways in 1947 upon my arrival from Germany, and I remember thinking what a glorious waste that was. When I was back and became a professor of technical physics, I learned something of the progress in automotive technology which lead to cars which were cheap and effective; we were asked about technical details by engineers of Daimler-Benz, and later I met the famous Hungarian Bareniy who has done so much for the safety of cars. By the efforts of the engineers and by the will of industrialists, and of the politicians, too, cars became available to many individuals. Public transportation lost in importance, and it was now possible to live far from one's place of work, and from railway stations. Housing locations changed correspondingly, and soon the car, which had been a convenience, became a necessity for many. In addition, whoever had a car, was tempted to use it to capacity, and this might explain the crowding of our cities and at least half the endless stream of vacationers abroad.

Now we have questions. First, is this development desirable? The answers will vary; my own suspicion is that less would have been better. Second, who has contributed to this development? The scientists yes, but their role is not decisive. The blame that falls on them can only be minor. The engineers, yes. But their role has been to design better cars, cheaper cars, safer cars, each of which aims is a good thing if there are to be cars at all. Industry, yes. Its task is to produce something that people want, to create work for many, and while doing this to survive. The politicians will encourage this because without industrial activities there cannot be economic growth and well being. And last but not least, the public, those who want to buy and use the products. Who is responsible? We shall have to come back to the scientists in this respect. But are the producers responsible? Or the public?

First, there is no responsibility in the sense: you must, or the law will punish you, with the exception that the producer and seller must be honest, and the product must be safe. Here is a small piece of technical responsibility for the scientists, and more for the engineers. Industry in a democracy is, within certain regulations, free to produce and sell what the consumer wants. This includes measures for safety and for the protection of the environment because this is included in the wishes of the population. The other responsibilities of the industry which are so often discussed in the media, are not defined by law but by reproaching them an exaggerated search for profit and lack of sense for the "true" needs of the people.

And the public? Everybody, again in a democracy, accepts the freedom of the citizens to decide what they want and how to spend their money. As a matter of fact, they alone decide in the end how many cars are sold and used in a country. The government cannot usually do much more than help to maximize this number. The question now is: is this as it should be? And this (if you allow me to continue my simplistic analysis a little further) must lead to the question: should the public want what it wants?

This is a difficult question. The answer should be yes because the citizen is free so long as he does not obstruct the freedom of others. However, it cannot be said that he is infallible; nobody is, and in addition everybody depends on information. In the case of cars this is a simple problem: the customer will first ask: is it an advantage for me to own a car? If the answer is positive, he will not worry about other problems such as: are there too many cars in Germany, and should I help by not buying one? I personally know only two persons who have given up their cars for this reason, and they are not even Greens. Or they might think: "one percent of the population are killed in motorcar accidents. I do not want to be part of this. When I weigh the advantage of using a car against the danger of killing myself or somebody else, my decision is clear." I would think that a number of people, especially older ones, follow this argument, but in percentages their number is negligible.

In general, however, the problem of weighing is paramount because each decision is not only a decision to do or allow something, but also a decision not to do or to forbid something else, and for both choices there are advantages and disadvantages. Let me try to discuss this point using my experiences in nuclear energy, limiting myself to the barest skeleton of the discussion. In the fifties and early sixties, public opinion was all in favor of nuclear energy as a convenient and cheap source of energy which would last much longer than the energy furnished by fossil fuels. It was known that there was a risk of accidents which would contaminate large areas with radioactivity so they had to be evacuated and could no longer be used for agriculture. But the risk, defined as damage times the probability per year for this accident, was calculated and considered to be sufficiently small compared to other industrial risks. I had to do with this at the beginning of the German efforts to maximize reactor safety. Since, this effort has greatly increased and now comprises more than one thousand persons in our country alone. There have been improvements in the evaluation, but in principle our early results are still valid. The largest accident will concern about 0.0002 percent of the earth's surface and about the same fraction of its population, and its probability should be around one per one million years per reactor. If one counts victims per year as damages like the insurance companies must, this is less than all other industrial risks. In the vicinity of a reactor, however, it is a spectacular and serious accident.

The accident of Chernobyl has confirmed the data about the accident (one must allow for large individual variations). It has not confirmed the probability figure but it is acknowledged that the conditions at Chernobyl were unique and no extrapolation to Western reactors is possible.

Another datum for the discussion: In 1961, I was in India as an official delegate, and there we learned about the deplorable living conditions and lack of work in this beautiful and cultured country. What can be done for the third world? This again has been a long discussion but one point that concerns the energy needs is uncontested: the population will grow, and raising the standard of living is considered a necessity. This, however, takes energy, and the predictions are that in fifty years, two or four times the present energy consumption will be needed. The problems are much less urgent now but this is serious for the future. If it is true, in addition, that the consumption of fossil fuels should be diminished or at least not be increased, for fear of dangerous climatic changes, this would mean that all energy sources including nuclear energy will be badly needed in fifty years even if all efforts at saving energy are made.

SCIENTIFIC MAN: CURSE OR BLESSING?

This is where weighing is demanded. And it means weighing with unknown weights. How does an advantage for the third world compare with an accident in an industrialized country? Or what is the weight of a single accident with maybe thousands dead and a territory of one thousand square kilometers lost, compared to one hundred thousand starving gradually each year, one by one? One might think that the answers are not too difficult but this is not true. Whoever has studied the problem knows that it has received great public attention, and this means that all possible theories, explanations, reproaches to all sides exist and are believed by many. Everybody by now must have learned that the public is unwilling to weigh or compare and that for any opinion it is true that a considerable fraction is liable to accept it. Relying on the wisdom of the public is not advisable. And in the public debate, many interests are at work today, including the political parties who depend on the good will of the voters. One of the great problems of our time is whether it will ever be possible to make the public discussion, which of necessity is a domain of the media, into a tool for a more complete and unbiased information of the public. This is why we must think twice whenever we read or hear that what the majority of the public want should be done.

Here are the big problems of our time. Blaming the scientists is not more than a search for scapegoats.

There is one last point. I remember a discussion in television with Edward Teller where one member of our parliament cried: "It is our wish that your ideas should have no influence on our destiny." Is there a danger that scientific thought will win over traditional ways of thinking, to the detriment of mankind? I have no authority to answer this question. I cannot resist, however, mentioning one point which should speak in our favor. When a scientist discovers something, or publishes a new theory, this may be true or false. He may have erred, but in most cases, this will soon come out. One reason is that the truths we look for are relatively simple. There may be uncertainties; to say that a statement is uncertain may be a true statement. We are accustomed to search for truth, and we use a principle which helps us to do so, namely the academic ethic which demands from us to be the first to doubt our results, to seek objections ourselves and to encourage objections by others. I admit that not all scientists adhere to this at all times, but still it is the basis of all scientific effort, and of the credibility of the scientists.

There is something else, too. Rational scientific thinking is limited to a small part of human knowledge and human activities. It cannot dominate where it is not valid. But where it is valid it should dominate in the sense that it should be taken into consideration whenever decisions are sought. Decisions can rarely be based on rational arguments alone. But they will be better if these arguments are not neglected.

A last and very important point: the rational and true arguments which a scientist can furnish concern his own field. When he leaves this field, as is his right as a citizen, we must be aware that his arguments are not more rational than those of others, and if he claims special authority for them, we must call this hubris or charlatanery. I should think that this hubris has contributed more than anything else to weaken the credibility of the scientists, and I am often tempted to call them a curse.

NOTES

1. As estimated by R. L. Mössbauer.
2. From personal communication with Alvin Weinberg.

AFTERWORD

POLITICS AND CULTURE

Robert H. Bork

The future prospects of liberal democratic societies must be estimated from the direction of changes that have already occurred. It is difficult to describe those changes without sounding like a curmudgeon. But my purpose is not to complain but to trace a progression. A few years back, Francis Fukuyama published the thesis that the world has now seen the victory of economic and political liberalism. Though it is not the case that every country has reached or is near that stage, it is the case that all ideological opposition to the liberal democratic society—primarily the Fascist and Communist alternatives—have been destroyed as living faiths. Sooner or later—Fukuyama gives himself a rather comfortable margin for error of 200 years—political and economic liberalism will triumph and we will see "the victory of the idea of the universal homogeneous state," and, one supposes, its realization. With the end of all ideological pretensions of representing a different and higher form of human society than liberal democracy, will arrive the end of history.

Not that Fukuyama is overjoyed at this prospect, for he says:

> The end of history will be a very sad time. The struggle for recognition, the willingness to risk one's life for a purely abstract goal, the worldwide ideological struggle that called forth daring, courage, imagination, and idealism, will be replaced by economic calculation, the endless solving of technical problems, environmental concerns, and the satisfaction of sophisticated consumer demands.

In fact, he concludes: "Perhaps this very prospect of centuries of boredom at the end of history will serve to get history started again."

It seems at least possible, however, that liberal democratic societies will prove unhappy in other ways than those suggested by Fukuyama and that they will do so for a reason he mentions in passing: "the emptiness at the core of liberalism [which] is most certainly a defect in the ideology." That, I think, is not stated strongly enough. There is an emptiness in the heart of liberalism that is so large a defect that it threatens the prediction of the universal and homogeneous state created by the victory of economic and political liberalism. The essence of modern liberalism would seem to be the absence of, indeed hostility to, any principle of transcendence. This leads to moral disorientation and that in turn to the loss of the sense of community and to the possibility of social disintegration. This is accompanied by the intense politicization of all aspects of the culture, which further fragments and divides us. For that politics, though it has a common theme, has no over-arching vision or program. It is merely the angry attack of left-liberalism at a thousand different and seemingly unconnected points. Indeed, if modern liberalism has a transcendent principle, it is a religion of politics, a belief that every subject is at bottom political, that politics is the means to salvation. The emptiness at the heart of liberalism consists in the belief that liberty and equality are ends in themselves and that nothing lies beyond them. That means that more liberty and more equality must constantly he demanded.

It is in this connection, I think, that Fukuyama makes a mistake. He speaks of the triumph of political parties that are "unabashedly pro-market and anti-statist" and then of

> an intellectual climate whose most "advanced" members no longer believe that bourgeois society is something that ultimately needs to be overcome. This is not to say that the opinions of progressive intellectuals in Western countries are not deeply pathological in any number of ways. But those who believe that the future must inevitably be socialist tend to be very old, or very marginal to the real political discourse of their societies.

Those who hold deeply pathological opinions in the United States are by no means a small band of "progressive intellectuals" but are rather an intellectual class numbering in the millions or tens of millions. They have been identified as the intellectual or knowledge class and, for reasons by now fairly well known, tend to be left of center. The class is defined by the fact that its members work with ideas—as academics, journalists, clergy and church staffs, bureaucrats, members of public interest organizations, and the like—not because they are particularly adept at intellectual endeavors. Perhaps a better name for them is Daniel Bell's happy phrase, a class of "semiskilled intellectuals" or Paul Johnson's name, "the chattering classes." What is important about them is not their intellect but their rapidly growing numbers, the opinions and values they hold, and their control of the cultural institutions that create and manipulate the symbols that define our lives.

Their potency has been enormously enhanced by the coming of age of the 60s generation which has now reached positions of influence and brought its radical ideological baggage along. Some of that generation once formed a political movement called the New Left. That collapsed as a movement but they are still the new left, in lower case. These people quite naturally went into universities, journalism, and other intellectual class professions, and they are far more active politically along strong ideological lines than any other group in our society.

It may be correct that this left does not believe that the future must inevitably be socialist since socialism is now so widely perceived as a fiasco that those who seek influence cannot advocate it, but that does not mean socialism may not arrive by increments through government programs enacted for different areas over a period of years. The impulse remains the socialistic impulse without the socialist program. The inability to articulate that or any program results in frustration, increased anger at traditional institutions and morals, hence a radicalism that appears unprogrammatic, and organization not into a political party but fragmentation into a myriad of single-issue groups. These people advance something very like a Marxist critique of bourgeois society and its institutions without a Marxist program or any vision of the society and institutions that should take their place. It is also true that this class is deeply hostile to bourgeois culture and is attempting to displace it. That is what creates the increasingly bitter war in our culture. As with their lack of a program for replacing capitalist institutions, the left has no vision of what should replace traditional, bourgeois culture. This may appropriately be called nihilism.

These people have filled the emptiness and boredom that lies at the heart of liberalism with a passionate politics of the left and hence one whose central feature is egalitarianism and the conviction that all subjects are at bottom political.

This new left displays characteristics that are thought by some observers to be contradictory. In many areas of life, primarily the moral and aesthetic, its philosophy is intensely libertarian, individualistic, and hence one of moral relativism. The community must not define moral aesthetic standards in any way, and government must keep hands off such matters. Yet in other areas, most notably those concerning race, ethnicity, and gender, the new left's philosophy is highly coercive and moralistic. Government must intrude massively into private life in such matters.

These may not be inconsistencies, at least from a severely egalitarian viewpoint. A leveler will think that, every man being as good as another, every man's morality is as good as any other's. Hence the community must not be allowed to enforce moral standards. But where innocent social and cultural factors produce inequality, government must counteract that and produce not simply equality of opportunity but equality of result. Equality of result has become an unpopular ideal in the economic sphere, essentially for the same reasons that socialism has lost its popular appeal, The demand has shifted to one of equality of result for groups and those groups are defined primarily by race, ethnicity, and sex. Income inequality may be acceptable in itself but each group must share proportionally in admission to universities, careers, employment, and promotion.

Both of these aspects of the left liberal program tend to destroy community and social morale. Both tend to social disintegration. Moral relativism informs the public that nothing, secular or sacred, is above desecration or entitled to community respect. Moralism in the service of equality of results denigrates the idea of individual merit, produces resentment between races and the sexes, and breaks society down into warring groups demanding entitlements. In the US this is not just a black-white problem. With the growth in our Hispanic and Asian-American populations, it is now a multiracial and ethnic problem.

These are not demands of the left that have proven futile. To a great degree these programs have succeeded politically and suffused our culture. Nor is the tendency new. It has been the trend of liberal democratic societies for a long time. James Fitzjames Stephen's, in *Liberty, Equality, Fraternity,* criticized these same trends in 1873. And they are, of course, much older than that. What is interesting is how far these trends have progressed in the 20th century and the further questions, have they any stopping point? And, if not, will the societies they produce continue to deserve the adjectives liberal and democratic?

We have in America an institution that is a good indicator of the changing balance in our cultural war, the conflict between intellectual class values and traditional or bourgeois values. That institution is the Supreme Court of the United States. It not only reflects trends but strongly reinforces them. For four decades now the Supreme Court has been to the left of the American center, though not so far left as the intellectual class. Nevertheless, the class to which the Court is closest is the intellectual class and that class's influence may easily be seen in the Court's work. That influence is more potent in the United States than in many other countries because we have a written Constitution that judges interpret and their interpretations supersede all other law. The fact that our Constitution is written has proved to be an inadequate safeguard against the transportation of elite values having nothing to do with the meaning of the documents' provisions into a judge-made constitutional jurisprudence. It is now regarded as a controversial if not reactionary position to think that the original understanding of those who made the Constitution law should guide the judge. The overwhelming majority of law school professors reject that idea out of hand.

There is an ongoing political struggle for control of the Court precisely because it can override democratic votes. Should the United Kingdom adopt a Bill of Rights to be enforced by judges, that step will both transform the nature of the judiciary and greatly increase the political power of intellectual class values. That is a prospect not to be contemplated without considerable apprehension. It is no accident, as our friend Lenin would have put it, that British intellectuals, including professors of law, favor a Bill of Rights for the United Kingdom.

The American Supreme Court's reflection of liberal intellectual class values is easily demonstrated. The two largest principles that tend to give society as a whole some cohesion, some sense of shared values and hence of community, are patriotism and religion. Liberalism is uninterested in these and, indeed, hostile to them, though both are values held by a majority of Americans.

The Supreme Court, quite without compulsion from the historic Constitution, has struck at the symbols of both patriotism and religion. I offer two examples. The Court invalidated the laws of forty-eight states and of the United States that prohibited the physical desecration of the American flag. Two decades ago that decision would have been inconceivable. Three of the most liberal Justices in our history—Chief Justice Warren and Justices Black and Fortas—a trio unlikely to be enshrined in any Conservative pantheon—stated vigorously that flag desecration was not a form of "speech" protected by the Constitution. But the steady absorption into our jurisprudence of a rampant individualism has shaped the evolution of constitutional doctrine. Increasingly, the individual must be allowed to express anything he wishes in any way he wishes to express it. A few weeks earlier, the Court held it a violation of the first amendment's prohibition of the establishment of religion for a local government to permit the display of a creche in a government building. Just three decades ago this too would have been an inconceivable decision.

These decisions are merely the culmination—or perhaps we have not yet seen the culmination—of a long line of cases hostile to community values and celebrating an individualism so untrammeled that it makes moral relativism a constitutional command. The Court has extended constitutional protection to pornography and regularly defeats communities' attempts to exercise some control over their moral environment. The Court a few years back, for example, threw constitutional protection around the behavior of a man who wore into a courthouse a jacket bearing words suggesting with a four-letter wordthat the reader perform an act of extreme anatomical implausibility with the Selective Service System. The Court's majority opinion asked, "How is one to distinguish this from any other offensive word?" and then made moral relativism dispositive by concluding that "[O]ne man's vulgarity is another's lyric."

More recently, four members of the Court, in voting to strike down the application of a penal statute to homosexual sodomy, subscribed to the startling proposition that it is "a moral fact that a person belongs to himself and not others nor to society as a whole." If there is a class of "moral facts," this assuredly is not one of them. This is a statement of individualism so severe that no parent and no citizen can accept it without standing convicted of the deepest irresponsibility. But it does not stand alone in the Court's jurisprudence. Among the constitutional rights Justices have invented to free the individual from moral regulation are the following: the right to privacy, the right to dignity, the right to be left alone, and the right not to conform. All of these are invented rights, nowhere to be found in the actual Constitution, and hence illustrate in pure form the influence upon the Court of modern liberalism's moral relativism.

This may be seen throughout our culture. We had a furor in Washington because a gallery supported by the government with taxpayers' money canceled an exhibition of the photographs of Robert Mapplethorpe, an exhibition that featured such art as a photograph of one naked man urinating into the mouth of another. Another show contained Andres Serrano's *Piss Christ*, the photograph of a crucifix in a bottle of the artist's urine. The uproar is not over whether such exhibits may be banned, which is what the argument used to be about, but whether the government has a right to withhold funding from such displays. Similarly, there is a musical group calling itself Dead Kennedys that sings lyrics like "I kill children, I love to see them die." There is no thought of banning such material. Instead, the question is whether it is allowable even publicly to express disapproval of it. One is tempted to agree with Richard John Neuhaus's characterization of ours as a "sub-pagan culture."

The Supreme Court has reflected the other tendency of intellectual class opinion as well: egalitarianism. The Civil Rights Act of 1964, in its text and in the promises of its sponsors, flatly forbids racial or sexual preferences of any kind. Yet a majority of the Supreme Court has read the statute to allow just such preferences for those who are neither white nor male, and it has interpreted the law in a way that presses employers to adopt quota systems in self-defense. When the Court pulled back only slightly from its position favoring quotas, the outcry from the liberal press, civil rights groups, and the intellectual class generally was one of outrage. Indeed, the dissenting Justices effectively accused the majority of racism. Much of this is pure moral intimidation designed to stop the Court from going further and, if possible, to make it recant. The vote for even moderate adjustment was, after all, only five to four. Interestingly enough, so powerful is the incantation of the phrase "civil rights," and so united is liberal sentiment, especially in the media, in favor of racial and sexual quotas, that there was little movement in Congress to correct the Court's original obvious misreading of the 1964 Civil Rights Act to allow such preferences.

Transcendent principles come in various sizes, of course, and among them is the belief that each intellectual discipline, each field of academic study, has proper standards of intellectual rigor and intellectual honesty. No group knows better than this that those principles are under attack and in retreat everywhere—from law to history to literary studies to the social sciences, most certainly in religion and journalism, even to some extent in the natural sciences. A few years back, some paleontologists who doubted that the extinction of the dinosaurs had been caused by the impact of a meteor reported that their careers were threatened. The theory that the meteor threw up dust clouds that blocked the sun's light was seen by some of its proponents as support for the idea that a nuclear exchange would have the same effect on the planet, and hence as supporting even unilateral nuclear disarmament. The dissenters to the dinosaur theory were contemptuously called "militarists." Many of these fields have been largely overrun by the view that they must be politicized and that standards of rigor and honesty are themselves political weapons designed to perpetuate the dominance of a corrupt and oppressive western culture and, in particular, the dominance of white males. The insistence upon the equality of all cultures and equality of results for all groups means that traditional standards must be displaced. And since equality is the main creed of the political religion, it is essential that new victim groups constantly be identified.

Selection for the editorial boards of law reviews, to take but one example, was until quite recently based entirely upon merit as demonstrated by grades or a writing competition. At one prestigious law school after another, selection is now done on the basis of quotas for "disadvantaged groups." These are currently defined by race, ethnicity, gender, physical handi-caps, and even sexual orientation. It is impossible to guess what victim groups the ingenuity of the egalitarians will identify next. But it is clear that the intellectual standards of this discipline, as of many others, count for less and less.

It is possible that these matters are cyclical, that our leading intellectual and cultural institutions will find a new era of integrity. In England, after all, the dissoluteness of the Regency was followed, unpredictably, by the rectitude of the Victorian era. The argument for that might rest upon the observation that the excesses we are witnessing are caused by the arrival of the 60's generation at middle age and at posi-tions of power and influence in all of our intellectual and

220

cultural institutions. Perhaps, then, we are living in an aberrational period, one that will pass as the 60's generation goes to
its reward.

But it seems unlikely that this period is wholly aberrational.
For one thing, a great deal of damage has been done and may
not be reversible. The left-liberals control the most prestigious
institutions, the cultural heights, which enables them to recruit
and socialize many of the best of the next generation, or at
least those most likely to join the intellectual class. In any
event, the 60's generation was not a reversal but a convulsive
acceleration of trends already long in motion. Many liberal
faculty members recognized that fact, some of them sadly. At
the time of the Columbia University student turmoil, it is said
that Lionel Trilling urged the faculty to accept what was taking
place, saying, "These are our proper children." It is very
probable that he was right. If so, the passing into history of the
60's generation may mean at best the slower continuation of
the processes we have been discussing.

It is always dangerous to extrapolate present trends to
predict a future state. While the intellectual class dominates
the cultural heights, it is also true that a majority of Americans—and, I would guess, a majority of the citizens of most
liberal democratic societies—reject intellectual class values.
Moreover, in recent years there has come into existence a
significant number of dissident members of the intellectual
class—in America, we call them, rather inaccurately,
neo-conservatives—and many of them are quite young. If the
great body of the citizenry can be made aware of the cultural
war that rages around them, there is a good chance that the
progress of left-liberalism can be checked.

But let us suppose that it is not checked. What then of the
future of liberal democratic societies? Will they be concerned
only with "economic calculation, the endless solving of
technical problems, environmental concerns, and the satisfaction of sophisticated consumer demands?" That will not be
true if the society is highly ideological and politicized, if it is

split into groups fighting for group entitlements, and if the results of moral relativism offend those with traditional values. That describes a fragmented, fractious, polarized and angry society and one unlikely to be stable.

In a wealthy but unhappy society, moreover, there is a considerable likelihood that human evil will find a new organizing principle, that will threaten both liberalism and democracy. The great organizing principles of evil in this century—Communism and Fascism—are surely not the only ones the mind of man can devise. There is in man a longing for the transcendent and the emptiness at the heart of liberalism is an invitation to some new transcendent principle to fill it. The nature of that principle it is too soon to say. We may hope that the rise of the subclass of dissident intellectuals and the existence of groups like this mean that there is at least a chance that the new principle will be benign.

NOTES ON CONTRIBUTORS

ROBERT H. BORK is a lawyer and John M. Olin scholar in legal studies at the American Enterprise Institute for Public Policy Research in Washington, D.C. He is a former federal judge and was nominated for the U.S. Supreme Court in 1987, with confirmation denied by the U.S. Senate. He was professor of law at Yale Law School (1962-1975). He is author of numerous books and articles including: *The Anti-Trust Paradox: A Policy at War with Itself* (1978) and *The Tempting of America: The Political Seduction of the Law* (1990).

ANTHONY DE JASAY is an economist and political philosopher who left his native Hungary in 1948. He was a Research Fellow at Nuffield College, Oxford. He later entered banking and finance in Paris and in 1979 took early retirement in France. He is the author of: *The State* (1985), *Social Contract Free Ride: A Study of the Public Goods Problem* (1989), and *Choice, Contract, Consent: A Restatement of Liberalism* (1991).

GEORGE P. FLETCHER is Cardozo Professor of Jurisprudence, Columbia University School of Law. His many publications include *Rethinking Criminal Law* (1978), *A Crime of Self-Defense: Bernhard Goetz and the Law on Trial* (1988), and *Loyalty: An Essay on the Morality of Relationships* (1993).

HEINZ MAIER-LEIBNITZ is emeritus Professor of Technical Physics at the Technical University of Munich. Since 1952 he has been involved in research and teaching in Atomic physics, nuclear physics, and solid state physics. He was the first director of the Institute Laue Langevin in Grenoble (1967-1972), president of the International Union of Pure and Applied Physics (1972-1975), and president of the Deutsche Forschungsgemeinschaft (1974-1979).

THE BALANCE OF FREEDOM

ALLAN H. MELTZER is University Professor of Political Economy and Public Policy, Carnegie-Mellon University and Visiting Scholar, American Enterprise Institute. He is the author or co-author of *Political Economy* (1991), *Monetary Economics* (1989), *Money and the Economy: Issues in Monetary Analysis* (1993) and other books and articles. He is co-editor of the *Carnegie-Rochester Conference Series on Public Policy*.

ROGER MICHENER has been professor of law and social thought at the University of Chicago, at Princeton University, and at Tokyo University.

ANDRZEJ RAPACZYNSKI is Professor of Law at Columbia University Law School. He served as an advisor to the Parliaments of Poland and Russia, helping to draft new constitutions and co-directs (with Roman Frydman) the Privatization Project of the Central European University.

WALTER H. RÜEGG is Professor of Sociology emeritus at the University of Berne (Switzerland). He has been lecturer and professor at the University of Zurich (1950-1961)and the University of Frankfurt (1961-1973), where he was also rector (1965-1970). He has lectured internationally, and has served as president of numerous academic organizations. His publications include: *Cicero und der Humanismus* (1946), *Antike Geisteswelt* (4th edition, 1980), *Soziologie* (8th edition, 1975), *Anstoesse* (1973), and *Bedrohte Lebensordnung* (1978). He is General Editor of *A History of the University in Europe* (1992-).

EDWARD SHILS is Professor of Social Thought and Sociology at the University of Chicago and honorarary fellow of Peterhouse, Cambridge. He is founder and editor of *Minerva: A Review of Science, Learning, and Policy*.